Dreams and Destinies

Dreams and Destinies

Marguerite Yourcenar

TRANSLATED BY
DONALD FLANELL FRIEDMAN

St. Martin's Press
New York

ISBN 0-312-21289-5

Yourcenar, Marguerite.
  [Songes et les sorts. English]
  Dreams and Destinies / Marguerite Yourcenar ; translation by
 Donald Flanell Friedman.
      p. cm.
   ISBN 0-312-21289-5
   I. Friedman, Donald Flanell. II. Title.
 PQ2649.08S613 1999
 154.6'3—dc21   99-14215
                                                         CIP

Book design by Acme Art, Inc.

First Edition: November, 1999
10 9 8 7 6 5 4 3 2 1

In the waking state, men share a world in common, but asleep, each possesses a separate universe.

Heraclitus of Ephesus

During certain periods of my life, I have noted my dreams; I have discussed their significance with the priests, philosophers, and astrologers. This aptitude for dreaming, blunted for years, has been restored to me in the course of these months of death-struggle; the events of the waking state seem less real, sometimes less important than these dreams. If this larval, spectral world, wherein the vapid and absurd flourish even more abundantly than on earth, offers us an idea of the soul's condition when separated from the body, I will doubtlessly spend my eternity in regretting the exquisite control of the senses, the perspectives readjusted by human reason. And yet, it is not without suavity that I delve into these shadowy realms of dream; I possess there, momentarily, certain secrets which soon escape me; I drink there from the wellsprings. The other day, I was at the oasis of Ammon, the evening of the hunt for the great, wild beast. I was filled with alacrity; everything occurred as it had during the time of my strength: the wounded lion fell down, then arose; I hastened to dispatch it. But this time, my terrified horse hurled me to the ground; the horrible, bloody mass rolled over me; claws lacerated my chest; I came back to myself in my room in Tibur, calling out for help. Even more recently, I again beheld my father, although he seldom enough occupies my thoughts. He was lying down on his sickbed, in a room in our villa in Italica, from which I withdrew immediately after his death. On his table, he had a vial filled with a sedative potion that I entreated him to give me. I awakened before he had a chance to answer. I am astonished that the majority of men are so fearful of ghosts when they so readily accept speaking to the dead in their dreams.

Memoirs of Hadrian
(1951)

At the bedside of the ill, he often had the opportunity of hearing dreams told. He had also had his own dreams. One was almost always satisfied with deriving omens, sometimes true, from these visions, since they reveal the sleeper's secrets, but he told himself that, above all else, this play of the mind given free rein could provide us with information about the way in which the soul perceives things. He enumerated the qualities of substance seen in dream: lightness, impalpability, incoherence, total freedom in respect to time, the instability of the forms of external appearance which causes each one to be many people and the many to be reduced to one, an almost Platonic sense of reminiscence, an almost unbearable impression of necessity. These apparitional categories strongly resembled what the hermetists claimed to know about existence from beyond the tomb, as if the world of death prolonged for the soul the world of night. Yet, life itself, scrutinized by a man ready to leave it, also acquires the strange instability and the bizarre ordinance of dreams. He passed from one state to the other, as if from the registrar's office, where he was interrogated, to his carefully bolted cell, and from his cell to the courtyard covered in snow. He saw himself at the doorway of a narrow turret where his Swedish Majesty gave him lodging at Vadstena. A great elk which Prince Erik had pursued in the forest the day before now stood facing him, motionless, patient, like an animal waiting for help. The dreamer felt that it was his mortal duty to hide, to rescue the wild creature, but without knowing by what contrivance to make him cross the threshold of this human refuge. The elk was a shining, damp black, as if it had come to him from across a stream. Another time, Zeno was in a barge that ran from a river into the open sea. It was a brilliant day of sunlight and wind. Fish by the hundreds slipped and swam around the stem, swept away by the current and outrunning it in turn, proceeding from sweet water to salt water, and this migration and this departure were filled with joy. But dreaming became unnecessary. Things assumed of their own accord those colors that they possess in dreams only and that recall the pure green, purple, and white of alchemical nomenclature: an orange, which suddenly appeared one day to luxuriously adorn his table, blazed for a long time like a golden orb; its perfume and savoriness also held a message. Over and over again, he was sure he heard a solemn music, resembling an organ's, if only an organ's strains could unfold in silence; the mind, rather than the hearing, received these sounds. With fingertips, he brushed the slack roughness of a brick covered with lichen and believed that he was exploring entire worlds. One morning, while going round the yard with his warden, Gilles Rombaut, he glimpsed on the uneven pavement a layer of transparent ice, beneath which a vein of water ran and thrilled. The slender flow sought and found its declivity.

The Abyss
(1968)

Contents

A Note on the Translation

In a letter of intent dated November 2, 1970, Marguerite Yourcenar stated her wish that, in the eventuality that she, herself, could not complete recension of *Dreams and Destinies,* which she planned to expand with later commented dreams, the book should at least be republished with selected passages from the *Memoirs of Hadrian* and *The Abyss* provided as epigraphs that would express her essential thoughts on dreams. The Pléiade edition follows Marguerite Yourcenar's exact indications for the placement of annotations to the original 1938 preface, which amplify the text with authorized commentary (and appear here as footnotes). The body of the 1938 preface remains essentially the same, with slight modifications in light of handwritten correction sheets and a copy of the original edition in which Grace Frick collated the author's changes. The most telling of these is the shift from the evocation of death as the "great, dark certainty" in the 1938 text to the present reflection, "the great, dark uncertainty."

Finally, the Pléiade edition of *Dreams and Destinies* is greatly enriched with the author's working notes in progress for the revision of the book. These sometimes fragmentary texts are always fascinating and reveal the play of a great mind at work on the enigma of dream. The file includes comparisons of the dream and afterlife states in the Tibetan *Book of the Dead,* as well as a collection of dream recitations, some dated from 1965-1979, which form another cohesive suite exploring oneiric experience in a different register from the original sequence. As explained in the section of this translation titled "File on *Dreams and Destinies,*" the material included derives from notebooks in the archives of Editions Gallimard and, when indicated, in the Houghton Library of Harvard University. The Harvard text "Concerning a System of Dreams and Yogic Exercises" is provided in an expanded form in this translation, with the gracious permission of Marguerite Yourcenar's estate and the Houghton Library. All English renditions of cited passages from Marguerite Yourcenar's work are this translator's own.

Translator's Acknowledgments

I would like to express my deep gratitude to Michael Flamini of St. Martin's Press, New York, who from the outset shared my enthusiasm for Marguerite Yourcenar's rare dream narratives and the spiritual journey they unfold. My appreciation as well to Jean Lunt of the Petite Plaisance Trust, who was most kind and encouraging when I first inquired about the possibility of presenting this work to readers of English. This endeavor was realized with the gracious permission of Yannick Guillou of Editions Gallimard, Marc Brosselet, and the members of the Marguerite Yourcenar Estate. My thanks as well to Hugues Pradier of the Pléiade editions. I am grateful to all for their generosity, kindness, and confidence in my efforts. To Mr. Guillou, I would like to express my special thanks for his cordiality, support, and kind faxed responses to questions. I would like to mention as well Anne-Solange Noble and her colleagues in the foreign rights department at Gallimard. Madame Noble worked adroitly with Mr. Flamini to realize this book. My gratitude also to Alan Bradshaw at St. Martin's Press for his cogent editing and for seeing this book to press. Special thanks to Sylvie Zannier-Betts, who was my first contact in the rights' department and whose energetic warmth was heartening.

The process of translating Marguerite Yourcenar's dreams has been a journey for me as well, one that has brought me into contact with many wonderful people. I would like to express immense gratitude to the librarians of the Houghton Library, Harvard University, Leslie Morris, curator of manuscripts, and Jennie Rathbun of the Houghton Reading Room, whose good offices made it possible for me to read enriching texts and supplement the final section, "Files on *Dreams and Destinies*." My special appreciation to Bonnie B. Salt, cataloger of manuscripts, who was engaged with the Marguerite Yourcenar papers for years and most generously shared her index and enthusiasm with me. I would like to express my gratitude to Marc-Etienne Vlaminck of the Centre Internationale de Documentation Marguerite Yourcenar at the Archives de Bruxelles for so warmly and generously sharing his immense expertise. The essays and information he kindly sent have enriched my understanding of Marguerite Yourcenar's international impact. My thanks to Jane Block, extraordinary Belgicist and art historian, whose work provides inspiration. At home in South Carolina, I had the opportunity to meet the dedicated members of the Rock Hill Arts Council. Their warmth and true interest in this translation in its initial stages were sustaining. I am most appreciative for the grant of the Rock Hill Arts Council that supported the translation in progress and for that of the Research Council at Winthrop University, my academic home now for a decade, at the culmination of the book.

These translations of dreams were begun during a period of convalescence following surgery when I was surrounded by the radiant warmth of treasured friends and colleagues, uplifted by their concern. Such friendship has brought me joy and delight. Among these friends, I would like to express appreciation to Lorraine Terzo-Raynor for her preparation of the manuscript, a process filled with her care, discernment, and bright spirits. Always, my deepest gratitude to Elaine Flanelle Friedman, ever wise and an attentive listener as the dreams were transcribed into English. Admiration, always, for Friederike Zeitlhofer.

I think of three deceased mentors, treasured friends who valued the dream and literature. Anna Balakian, dedicated to the comparative study of literature, Luc Fontainas, scholar and connoisseur, and Paul Willems, writer and sage, have imparted knowledge and experience. They will remain guides in life and art.

These translations are reverently
dedicated to the memory of my mother and father.

Reflections on the Dreamed Life of Marguerite Yourcenar

Les Songes et les sorts, Dreams and Destinies, was first published by Grasset in
the Paris of 1938, on the verge of the devastating war years, in an edition
of 3,000 copies with bold, spacious type, each section blazoned with the
chimerical image of Pegasus, suggestive of the hermetic and transporting
nature of this sojourn in the shadow-realm of dream. In an interview
published in 1980, the year she became the first woman elected to the
Académie Française, Marguerite Yourcenar asserted her wish to add to the
book, expanding discussion of the nature of dream and supplementing the
original dream sequences with the nocturnal explorations of her later years.[1]
Unfortunately, the author was unable to realize this project before her death
and *Les Songes et les sorts* was republished only posthumously in the 1991
Pléiade volume *Essais et Mémoires,* following certain indications of the author
and including her working notes as a "Dossier," suggestive of directions the
work might have taken. *Les Songes et les sorts* occupies a modest position in
the final section of the Pléiade volume. In *"Textes Oubliés,"* "forgotten" or
"neglected texts," a nomenclature that Yourcenar could have well
appreciated as a protective concealment for this series of Orphic underworld voyages, the author delves into her inner world and returns with

dream-artifacts presented to the reader, laid out like tarot cards that tell the tale of her fate, arranged and descriptively labeled like pictures at an exhibition—"The Keys to the Church," "The Blue Water," "The Young Girl Who Weeps," "The Pathway Beneath the Snow"—neutral titles which designate without preparing us for the alluring and dangerous vortex of the dream recounted, the breath-taking drama of dissolution or regeneration found in each soulscape. Though a "forgotten text," this subtle and secretive book, at once intensely personal and veiled as are all hermetic texts, is a pivotal work in the Yourcenar canon, overlooked perhaps because of its literary nonconformism and blurring of genre distinctions, posing a diffi-culty of classification as it shifts from essayistic prose in the preface to mantic revelation of dream, limning a rare nocturnal self-portrait in twenty-two parts, each with its particular climate yet clearly interrelated to form a sequence of mythic quests for self-regeneration and recovery from the rejection of a lover who has become the absent God.[2] Such published narrations of dreams, presented neither randomly nor chronologically as would be the case in a dream journal that any of us might keep to chart our spiritual progress or spiritual temperature, but *arranged,* definitively com-posed as a book to provide maximum reverberation, contrast, and intersec-tion between the dreams, must ultimately be considered one of the most intimate and daring, though least conventional forms of autobiography.[3] As such it reveals the unguarded play of a mind liberated from the conceptual constraints of consciousness and lays bare the distilled essence of the author's profound selfhood, her interior geography normally hidden from observation.

Certainly, accounts of haunting dreams expressive of essential being or life experience are prominent in autobiographies and published journals, and modalities of dream experience have been determinant in literary creation in successive movements beginning with romanticism, a matrix of Yourcenar's dream book just as it was for the quite divergent experiments of her contemporaries, the surrealists. Influential for the surrealists and for Yource-nar, Baudelaire discusses in *Les Paradis artificiels* the miraculous nature of sleep and dream, "ce voyage aventureux de tous les soirs" [the adventurous voyage that takes place every evening], adding the depth of wonder and mystery, the *frisson* of the unknown, to quotidian existence.[4] The dream voyage is adven-turous, precisely because its course is uncharted, the destination never determined in advance. The dream is a separate and parallel life which inflects and shapes waking perception and provides intimations of otherworldly experience, as the romantic Nerval suggests in *Aurélia,* a novelistic imbrication of confession, hallucination, and dream that comprises a desperate search for salvation carried out in an oneiric register:

> Le sommeil occupe le tiers de notre vie. Il est la consola-
> tion des peines de nos journées . . . mais je n'ai jamais
> éprouvé que le sommeil fût un repos. Après un engourd-
> issement de quelques minutes une vie nouvelle com-
> mence, affranchie des conditions du temps et d'espace, et
> pareille sans doute à celle qui nous attend après la mort.[5]

> [Sleep takes up a third of our lives. It is the consolation for
> the toil of our days . . . but I have never found sleep to be
> a form of repose. After a few minutes of torpor, a new life
> begins, freed from the constraints of time and space,
> identical, no doubt, with the one awaiting us after death.]

As an initiation into lethal mysteries, a preparation for the disembodied state, and a search for a deified lost love, Nerval's dream voyage in *Aurélia* adumbrates Yourcenar's transcriptions.

In the wake of romantic explorations of the strangeness of dreams, their quicksilver transformations and distortions, their sudden shifts of setting and intermingling of the ordinary and untoward, writers of various stylistics have cultivated the dream messages of the irrational as a means of realizing new creative processes. Notwithstanding the force of dream in modern literature, books formed entirely of dream recitations, entirely devoted to these fragments of our nocturnal experience, remain a rarity. For Yourcenar, the dream transcriptions in *Les Songes et les sorts* are not a means, not creative limbering exercises to infuse other literary work, but an end product and creation. The grouping of significant dreams narrated, as Yourcenar asserts in her preface, without the practical end of analysis and without explanation of objective circumstances that may infuse the dreams is a curiously oblique and, therefore, liberating form of autobiography. The author invites the reader, anonymous stranger, to wander a picture gallery of the soul, contemplating the mechanisms and prismatic intricacies of dreams as refracted through the mind of one particular artist-dreamer, who has no responsibility to reveal the skein of life events which may be transformed into the more complexly interwoven strands of memory and desire in the dreams. We have, of course, the revelation of biographer Josyane Savigneau that Yourcenar's thwarted passion was for the writer André Fraigneau, to whom she dedicated the proximate collection of narratives of passion *in extremis* (which uses legendary characters as mouthpieces), the 1936 *Feux* [*Fires*].[6] In this volume published in the year that the dream transcriptions were completed, the author added the epigraph "To Hermes," thus coding the identity of the object of her longing as the God-psychopomp and patron of hermetists who bears dreams and leads souls to the underworld. Certainly, this life fact is telling but not essential to our appreciation of the dreams, intrinsically beautiful and mesmeric in their unfolding of subterranean experience and the erotic wound within their own register. Yourcenar herself presents the salient information in her preface when she states that dreams of the type recounted in her cycle are most frequently induced by crisis and extremity:

> . . . certaines aspirations mystiques, certaines renonce-
> ments, certaine dangereuse atmosphère de pure douleur
> ou de pure solitude sont favorables à l'enfantement des
> rêves hallucinés . . .[7]

> [. . . certain mystical aspirations, certain renunciations, a
> certain dangerous atmosphere of pure suffering or pure
> solitude are favorable to the emergence of hallucinated
> dreams . . .]

And she asserts in the preface, "Tous, nous n'avons jamais tant rêvé que dans nos périodes de désir, ou de douleur, qui n'est qu'un désir blessé."[8] [We have all of us never dreamed so abundantly as during our periods of longing, or of pain, which is but a wounded longing.] In an undated, handwritten working note for revision, Yourcenar reveals, "Les rêves rapportés dans *Les songes* . . . se situent à l'intérieur d'un moment de ma vie entièrement occupé par un intense et violent amour."[9] [The dreams reported in *Dreams and Destinies* . . . are set inside a moment of my life completely obsessed with an intense and violent love.] Yet, the 1938 sequence is offered without explicit reference to the author's diurnal activity and preoccupations and, precisely for this reason, the aesthetic pleasure afforded the reader is not that of conventional autobi-ography with its reportage or collage of experience, its elaboration of events, encounters, and spiritual conversions, but a delectation similar to that afforded by short fiction or the prose poem. The dream *transcription* is not a prose poem, but like the familiar literary form, it provides epiphanies through perception and explores constellations of mood, spiritual climate, and patterns of imagery in a cohesive narrative. In transcribing dreams, Yourcenar eschews explicative psychology in favor of the adventures of Psyche, the soul itself, the dreams being the fabric woven from the soul's substance. It suffices to unfurl and display the dream tapestries in order to reveal psychic essence.

The confessional and oblique aspects of Yourcenar's oneiric autobiography may best be understood in comparison with her more canonical memoirs, the tripartite *Labyrinth of the World,* written after the novels that established her fame. Here again, the self active in the world remains veiled in favor of more subtle disclosures. In *Labyrinth,* Yourcenar extracts herself, exploring, rather than her own peripatetic life, the ancestral past of her maternal and paternal families, the centuries of concatenation of destiny leading to her birth. This is, in essence, a biographical prolongation of her work as a novelist, engaged in imaginative restitution of the historical past. As a memoir, the author-narrator's being is reflected in the faceted mirrors of myriad other lives which preceded her own and which she explores, as she would a fictive historical life, through documentation and intuition. In this light, the earlier *Dreams and Destinies* is the more autobiographical text; though also turning away from the outward events of her life, Yourcenar does give vent to a confessional impulse by raising the curtain of her inner theater and transcribing the scenarios of the masques performed there. As oneiric autobiographer, Marguerite Yourcenar is both actress and audience of her private nocturnal theater; as transcriber, our guide as well as the protagonist with whom the reader identifies, following and experiencing, through the mediation of her language, the shape-shifting and unmediated visions of sleep, the magic that informs them.

The title of Marguerite Yourcenar's collection reveals her basic program and suggests various aspects of the mantic aura of dream. The selection of numinous and recurrent dreams experienced between the ages of twenty-eight and thirty-three, an oneiric compression of five years into a single moment, establishes parity, as the interplay *Songes-sorts* makes explicit, between dreams and destinies, plural. Each significant dream expresses parcels of the dreamer's essential singularity, while the orbit of dreams hints at the essential multiplicity of selfhood, a harmony of continuous and metamorphic being in keeping with the alchemical motto, *Unum sum et multi in me* [I am one and many at the same time.][10] With the seemingly limitless distribution of dream roles, our dreams are realms of possibility, suggesting a plurality of destinies rather than the shackled constraint of our daily condition; the dream compensates, restoring the liberty, the potentiality of selfhood. Each dream exerts for its recipient the fascination of magic, perhaps even of malefice in the dangerous dreams, since both fate and magic spells are inherent meanings of the highly charged word *sorts,* which also denotes in French the process of oracular divination, the casting of lots, and chance, appropriate to the dream, a random visitation impossible to foresee. For the word *dream* in her euphonious title, Yourcenar chooses *songe* rather than *rêve,* interchangeable in modern French and throughout the preface, but the former maintaining a suggestive link with its sixteenth-century origins, a nocturnal vision in the tradition of the classical *somnium,* for Macrobius, the enigmatic dream "that conceals with strange shapes and veils with ambiguity the true meaning of the information being offered. . . ."[11] The enigmatic dreams expressive of destiny are those which we would label archetypal or mythic, formulations which Yourcenar eschews in her preface in favor of lyrical or hallucinated dreams, an aesthetic terminology implicitly measuring the complexity of significant dreams against the standard of the multivalent artwork. In both art and dream, image is substituted for reality, the former fixed and the latter quintessentially evanescent, most often lost upon awakening or soon thereafter. But for Marguerite Yourcenar, a salient quality of the lyrical or hallucinated dreams, those possessing artistic dimension and those which are fateful, momentous, is that they do not vanish like the majority but remain engraved in our memory over the years and constitute, alongside a scattering of diurnal experiences of beauty and awe, part of our inner treasure. Other great artistic-dreamers concur. Luis Buñuel, for example, lists some fifteen recurrent dreams which have followed him throughout life, "like faithful traveling companions."[12] J. B. Priestly insists that among all the countless inconsequential and disposable dreams, we are each allotted our share of the magic and indelible:

> These dreams, which may bring us anything from terror to rich absurdity, seem to me to belong to a different order of dreaming. They do not come from the ragbag or rubbish disposal department, always offering us the instantly forgettable. They seem to me to be definite creations just as a produced play or a film is a definite creation . . .[13]

As Yourcenar explains in her prefatory discussion, this type of lasting dream, weightless phantasmagoria that enlarges our experience, is analogous to "cette baie magique du miroir" [that magic bay window of the mirror], affording the dreamer an introspective view of a soulscape and an expansive outward view of previously unexplored vistas.[14] The window-mirror is a privileged space of passage between realms, and a space of intangible, fleeting visions, reflected illusions which show us who we are and what we desire or fear. Essentially, the dream sequences are so many magic mirrors into which the author plunges her Narcissus-gaze, descrying teeming elisions of memory and desire, at times piercing the crystal into the luminous ideal. Like distorting mirrors, dreams in Yourcenar's formulation do not simply reflect, but correct, deform, or reverse the images of reality in a nonmimetic process of hallucination. Through its distortions, the dream demonstrates our innate capacity to fabricate private worlds, congruent with the artist's subjective reconstruction of the world in the artwork:

> Le miroir corrige les images, les déforme, ou les renverse: ces trois alternatives correspondent aux trois modes de rêves, selon qu'il s'agit des beaux songes qui restituent à la réalité son lustre idéal, des cauchemars qui nous renvoient de notre propre vie une image aussi grotesque qu'effrayante . . . et enfin de ces rêves ou les symboles inversés servent à dissimuler des vérités secrètes et dangereuses . . .[15]

> [The mirror corrects images, deforms, or reverses them: these three alternatives correspond to the three modes of dreams, whether a matter of beautiful dreams that restore an ideal radiance to reality, nightmares that return an image of our own life as grotesque as it is fearful . . . or finally those dreams wherein the inverted symbols serve to dissemble secret and dangerous truths . . .]

Restoring ideal luster to life or serving to disguise secret or dangerous truths—the first term echoes Baudelaire's assertion in *Les Paradis artificiels* that the dream is sometimes a mirror that shows man a rose-colored image of what he should or could possibly be, while the second echoes the definition of Macrobius's somnium, knowledge best imparted in symbolic guise.[16] These categories, shining visions of the ideal and beckoning visions of mystery which open our thoughts to conjecture, are also classifications of aesthetic experience. While the dreams recounted constitute for the author so many windows, partial or temporary openings into the labyrinth of her being, the readers of her texts peruse artifacts that bear witness to the parallels between dream and creative process, deriving aesthetic pleasure from the dream imagery or the volute play of language as the narrative unfolds, transposing private vision into shared discourse, the way a composer sets down notes to enable others to savor the harmonies he has imagined.

Yourcenar emphasizes that the dreamer, like the poet, gathers and links images, but does so to whisper essential secrets to himself:

> . . . l'expérience du rêveur n'est pas sans analogie avec celle du poète. . . . Le dormeur assemble des images comme le poète assemble des mots: il en use avec plus ou moins de bonheur pour parler de soi à soi-même.[17]

> [. . . the experience of the dreamer is not without analogy to that of the poet. . . . The sleeper assembles images the way the poet assembles words: he makes use of them more or less felicitously to speak about himself to himself.]

Dreaming is a private communication. Shared discourse versus self-discourse is the crucial difference between poetry and dream as elucidated by Yourcenar, imaginative writing being a dream with open eyes in which reader and writer participate, while the unmediated dream proper remains a private oracle for the sleeper's delectation, initiation, or instruction, a privileged means of self-communion. The artistic dimension of *Dreams and Destinies,* the fascination that the unusual book exerts, is due both to the sacral, initiatory aspect of the cycle, and, pervasively, to the language of mediation which the author forges as she strives to express essentially nonverbal visions in a shared communicative register.[18]

At the opening of the dream "The Wild Horses," Yourcenar furnishes a brief *ars poetica* on the nature of transforming dream into text:

> Les rêves les plus compliqués sont courts; ou plutôt, ils ne sont ni longs ni brefs, il se déroulent loin du temps. Par contre, toute description fidèle d'un rêve ne peut être que minutieuse et lente, puis qu'il s'agit d'accumuler les mots

qui permettront au lecteur . . . de s'introduire par le
détour d'analogies souvent bien lointaines au sein même
d'un monde étranger . . .[19]

[The most complex dreams are brief, or rather, neither
long nor short, but unfold outside of time. On the other
hand, any faithful description of a dream must necessarily
be slow and meticulous since this is a matter of amassing
the words that will allow the reader . . . to slip in through
a maze of often remote analogies to the heart of an
unknown world . . .]

Circumambulation rather than simple declarative discourse is most likely to
convey something of the mystery of the dream, a filmic flow outside of time.
Marguerite Yourcenar labels her style of transcription nonlinear and baroque,
since only a play of associational language can approach the intricate web of
the dream.[20] As baroque stylist, Yourcenar employs supple and sinuous
sentences that bend to her thought as they wend their way, attempting ever
more narrowly to encompass the elusive oneiric experience in an explorative
language of hesitancy, accumulating adjectives and luxuriant similes, vining
around the central mystery of timeless vision. This charged emotivity and
intent expressionism may well come as a shock for Yourcenar's readers in
English, most familiar with the chill, almost surgical restraint and concision,
imperturbability and smooth perfection of certain works of her fiction. In
Dreams and Destinies, Yourcenar's baroque abundance attempts to seize the
incomprehensible, while the intricate rhythms of the sentences with their
constant play of comparisons convey the process of noesis, experiential
knowledge gained through investigation.[21] The dream protagonist repeatedly
finds herself in unfamiliar worlds, in which she must weigh the circumstances
and surroundings. Illustrative in this regard is the opening of the initial dream,
"The Visions in the Cathedral," in which two simple sentences, "I am standing
in the transept of a church. Which church?" yield to an unexpected torrent of
imagery, conjuring possible sacred spaces, evoked and rejected, all simultaneously present and absent in thought. Similarly, in the "Pathway Beneath the
Snow," a single sentence evokes disparate seasons and places, a flower-filled
farmyard surrounded by snow, and a nocturnal isthmus of Corinth lit by a
ship's beacon. Flexible and complex, Yourcenar's prose reconstructs the
dream linguistically as an inner-world labyrinth in ramification, a nexus of

interrelation in which compressed layers of memories may be couched in polyphonic images. Calling her dream collection a suite, Yourcenar hints at both the baroque form, a system of diversity and coherence in which dances that vary in rhythm and mood but maintain a single key signature alternate in succession, as well as the suite in the modern sense (a condensation of an opera into orchestral selections which capture memorable moments of the larger work), fragmentary dream narratives extracted from a rich and continuous night music.[22]

As an inner voyage, the dreams of the 1938 sequence, mutually reflective in their recurrent colors, personae, architecture, landscapes, and reprisals of experience, form a set of variations on the interlocking themes of Eros and Thanatos. Yourcenar's Hadrian describes the divinity of the beloved, the single being "who haunts us like a piece of music."[23] Yourcenar's dream protagonist experiences self-dissolution and resurrection, leprous decay and baptismal renewal, while striving for the salvation of the beloved who assumes various guises until, in the culminating sacred marriage of "Love and the Linen Shroud," he is revealed as the illuminating Apollo, a regenerate Osiris bursting the chrysalis of his winding cloth, and Eros liberating the soul from the body for ecstatic union beyond life.[24] The 1938 dream sequence is charged throughout with what Yourcenar calls in the preface to her resurrection drama, *Alceste,* "the idea that death is not an end, but perhaps a beginning, a birth or voyage. . . ."[25] The fiery, whirling dance of death in which the protagonist's double, "The Young Girl Who Weeps," expires precedes the rapturous sacred marriage of the last dream. In *Dreams and Destinies,* experiences of mourning, severance, and peril alternate with experiences of ecstasy, beatitude, and transfiguration; in this regard, the dominant space of the church, recurring in four pivotal dreams that punctuate the cycle, is alternately sepulchral and a site of revelation in the protagonist's attempt to overcome death through love. By means of the hermetic dream experience and by means of its transposition into an imagistic and electrically charged literary cycle, the life of Marguerite Yourcenar, oneiric autobiographer, is doubled in myth in an initiatory process in which the reader witnesses the gestation of multidimensional selfhood. The dream instructs both author and reader in the spiritual truth of metamorphic being as Marguerite Yourcenar enters her text as narrator and sleeping protagonist, her doubles, guide figures, diverse characters and places manifest her inner cosmography. As an epigraph to the collection, Yourcenar cites Heraclitus in this regard: "In the waking state, men share a world in common, but asleep, each possesses a separate universe." Sleep is the alembic in which the true, the special climate of the soul is distilled. The separate universe provides us as well with an intuition of the sacred, defined by Yourcenar as "le sentiment de l'immense invisible et de l'immense incompréhensible qui nous entoure"[26] [an awareness of the vast unseen and unknown that encompasses our transitory being].

Since we are all dreamers and since many of us note and scrutinize our dreams which must necessarily remain a source of private reflection, the obvious question arises—why publish accounts of dreams? As an elitist response, one could assert that an artist's dreams possess interest since those engaged in refashioning the world are closest to the wellsprings of memory and creativity which sustain the dream and art. Such is certainly the case of Marguerite Yourcenar, an unsurpassed dreamer whose nocturnal *oeuvre* is richly glowing. And, as we have seen, there is the artistic experiment of forging an expression capable of conveying the nuance of the dream in literature. Underlying the project is a valorization of memory. The original preface to *Dreams and Destinies,* drafted by an already confident writer of fiction, a mature woman of abundant life experience and independence, sensitive as well to the seismic waves of impending cataclysm, has a markedly elegiac tone. It is as if the author somehow sensed that she was to leave behind the beloved European cities and relationships that had nurtured her inner life. The brief flashes of memory recounted at the end of the preface stand as a litany of illuminations within the dream of life. As a retrospective gaze in Yourcenar's early maturity, *Dreams and Destinies* is both a nostalgic farewell and a brave assertion that the intangible treasure of memory, the people, places, and dreams that respire within us, are forever one with us. Yourcenar, from youth an inveterate traveler for whom displacement was an essential mode of life, could not fail to savor the dream voyage. She must have realized in drafting this work that intangible dreams are, after all, the most portable of precious commodities. Memories of magic dreams are not only talismans, but also tokens of the hidden currents, the underlying depth of being. Recollection, in the tradition of the mysteries, is a source of realization of the divine origins of the soul and leads to awakening. In her "Orphic Verse," Yourcenar writes: "Gelid crystal, chill elixir,/The water of Memory fills my soul."[27]

Donald Flanell Friedman

Notes

1. Marguerite Yourcenar, *Les Yeux ouverts, entretiens avec Matthieu Galey* (Paris: Le Centurion, 1980), 108.

2. The only book-length study of *Les Songes et les sorts* and one that is brilliantly discerning and encompassing in its examination of modalities of dream as a dominant in Yourcenar's writing is Carmen Ana Pont's *Yeux ouverts, yeux fermés: la poétique du rêve dans l'oeuvre de Marguerite Yourcenar* (Amsterdam and Atlanta: Rodopi, 1994). Also of interest is Paul Pelkman's essay on experiences of solitude in *Les Songes et les sorts,* "Le Point de vue de la rêveuse," in *Bulletin de la Société Internationale d'Etudes Yourcenari-ennes* 5 (1989): 34-45. See also Patricia de Feyter, "Le Rêve, ce grand architecte," in *L'Universalité dans l'oeuvre de Marguerite Yourcenar I* (Tours: Société Internationale d'Etudes Yourcenariennes, 1994), 101-110; and Maria Cavazzuti, "*Les Songes et les sorts*: Mythologie du moi, miroir de l'universalité," in *L'Universalité dans l'oeuvre de Marguerite Yourcenar II* (Tours: Société Internationale d'Etudes Yourcenariennes, 1995), 107-110.

3. As recent oneiric autobiographies by magisterial writers of fiction, see the collection of dreams by Yourcenar's successor at the Académie Française, Dominique Rolin's *Train de rêves* (Paris: Gallimard, 1994), and William S. Burrough's *My Education: A Book of Dreams* (New York: Viking, 1995).

4. Charles Baudelaire, *Les Paradis artificiels* (Paris: Librairie Générale Française, 1972), 71.

5. Gerard de Nerval, *Aurélia* in *Oeuvres complètes III* (Paris: Gallimard, 1993), 749.

6. Josyane Savigneau, *Marguerite Yourcenar: Inventing a Life* (Chicago and London: University of Chicago Press, 1993), 92-104.

7. Marguerite Yourcenar, *Les Songes et les sorts* in *Essais et Mémoires* (Paris: Gallimard, 1991), 1536.

8. *Les Songes et les sorts,* 1537.

9. *Les Songes et les sorts,* 1611.

10. Marguerite Yourcenar inscribed this alchemical motto in her notebook, "Words and Symbols," housed in the Houghton Library, Harvard University, Cambridge, Mass., bMS FR 372.2 (542).

11. Macrobius, *Commentary on the Dream of Scipio* (New York: Columbia University Press, 1952), 90. For cogent discussion of the ancient, medieval, and Renaissance traditions informing Yourcenar's discussion of dream in her preface, see Carmen Ana Pont's *Les Yeux ouverts, les yeux fermés,* 24-31.

12. Luis Buñuel, *My Last Sigh* (New York: Knopf, 1983), 93.

13. J. B. Priestly, *The Happy Dream* (Andoversford: Whittingdon Press, 1976), 3.

14. *Les Songes et les sorts,* 1537.

15. *Les Songes et les sorts,* 1537.

16. Baudelaire, *Les Paradis,* 62.

17. *Les Songes et les sorts,* 1535.

18. In her 1980 interview, Yourcenar asserts, "dans les rêves de type magique, on ne s'entend pas parler, on voit quelque chose": vision rather than speech is an essential characteristic of the magic dream. *Les Yeux ouverts,* 111.

19. *Les Songes et les sorts,* 1575-1576.

20. In the *Les Yeux ouverts* interviews (47), Yourcenar speaks of her ornamental style of the period, influenced by baroque painters and poets.

21. For a discussion of the stylistics of baroque prose, see Alexander M. Witherspoon and Frank J. Warnke, *Seventeenth Century Prose and Poetry* (New York: Harcourt, Brace & Co., 1963). The introduction emphasizes the baroque "catalogues of approximate synonyms" and a sentence structure intended "to trace the very movement of the inquiring mind," 7.

22. *Les Songes et les sorts,* 1535; in the opening of the preface, Yourcenar compares her recurrent dreams to musical motifs, susceptible to infinite variation, 1534.

23. Marguerite Yourcenar, *Memoires d'Hadrien* in *Oeuvres romanesques* (Paris: Gallimard, 1982), 297.

24. Edgar Wind describes the erotic scenes on ancient sarcophagi in which "to die was to be loved by a god, and partake through him of eternal bliss," in *Pagan Mysteries of the Renaissance* (New Haven: Yale University Press, 1958), 130.

25. Yourcenar, *Théatre II* (Paris: Gallimard, 1971), 86.

26. Yourcenar, *Les Yeux ouverts,* 41.

27. Yourcenar, "Vers Orphiques," in *Les Charités d'Alcippe* (Paris: Gallimard, 1984), 27.

Dreams and Destinies

Preface

I wish herein to tell a few dreams, those which most intensely disturb or console a being who has dreamed considerably. Since adolescence (save for one or two exceptions, I scarcely remember my childhood dreams), I have been accompanied throughout my nocturnal life by a dozen disquieting or propitious dreams, as identifiable as musical motifs and susceptible, like them, to infinite variation. These dreams subdivide into groups, into clearly distinguishable families, similar to the provinces of some mysterious country that might only be visited with closed eyes. The reappearance of a selfsame character, of an object, of a detail of scenery, of the same sensation in my sleeping mind permit me to mark this or that nocturnal region where previous dreams had already transported me, but which I can never be sure of visiting again in the future. There is the region of dreams of remembrance, dominated by the figure of my dead father; the cycle of ambition and pride, which I have seldom wandered except during the nights of my twentieth year; the cycle of terror, the most primitive of all, populated with phantasmagoria of prisons, lepers, dragons, and torn-out hearts, but which I

*penetrate less frequently than before, since with time, dread diminishes like hope,
and we will doubtlessly grow old as reassured as paupers, who have no reason
to fear the theft of their misfortune.* * *There is the cycle of quest, concerned with
rediscovering the vestiges of a woman who has disappeared and changed into a
phantom; there is the cycle of death, which is replete with gardens and which
necessarily encompasses all the others, since it is impossible to either dream or
think profoundly without coming up against this great, dark uncertainty; there
is the cycle of the church, in which a cathedral is obsessively prominent, as
formidable and reassuring as the tomb, the night with its stars, the hollows of
the earth and of bodies; and sometimes this secret basilica is beheld from within,
strewn with the intermittent glint of candlelight and filled with a silence that
resembles solemn music, and sometimes it is viewed from outside and its double
doors refuse to part before the sleeping pilgrim, who lacks the key necessary to
penetrate its depths. And there is the dream of the pond, the only significant
dream that originates in childhood, and also the only one that recurs from one
year to another without the slightest change. And there is the dream of love,
which it is pointless to burden with commentary since the only profound exegetes
that this feeling has stirred until now are the organ and violoncello. These
various dreams do not proceed, moreover, without concluding mutual alliances:
the dreams of ambition, of love and death are frequently set within cathedrals,
and the dream of the pond is also a dream of sacred terror. And there is the dream
of melancholy happiness, recognizable in that it always unfolds beneath a
certain rose sky, and the dream of absolute bliss, which I have dreamed but once,
and where nothing transpires apart from an unforgettable blue color.*

*It is evident that I carefully set aside from these pages the physiological
dreams, too obviously caused or favored by a poor functioning of the stomach or
heart; and still more purposefully, I set aside those vague and muddled dreams,*

---

* Or yet again like the wealthy, who have amassed so much treasure that they say yes, in spite of all, to life. There are always two ways of seeing.

born of an indigestion of the memory, scarcely more than the shapeless residue
of trifling daily afflictions, usually as unworthy of having been dreamed as lived.
These occur the most frequently, for in the world of dreams just as in waking,
there are, unfortunately, more copper coins than gold pieces.

Likewise, I pass over in silence those purely sexual or postsexual dreams which
are little more than a simple assertion of desire (or of pleasure) by a sleeping man
or woman. Finally, I set aside those great dreams common to all, whose meaning
remains uncertain, but which appear to each of us in almost invariable guise and
confer upon us only emotions common to the entire nation of sleepers: dreams which
are like national highways and public gardens in the land of illusions. Whatever
might be, for example, the true significance of beautiful dreams of levitation, of
uneasy dreams of chase where doors open and shut around the fugitive outstretched
on his bed, and those unsettling dreams of exhibitionism in which the sleeper strolls
nude, astonished at not giving rise to scandal, these dreams, in and of themselves,
provide us with no more information about the sleeper's individual essence than a
metaphor sanctioned by usage enlightens us about the secret soul of the man who
utters it after ten thousand others.* On the contrary, what matters to me here is
the stamp of an individual destiny pressed upon the metal of dream, the inimitable
alloy that shared psychological or sensual elements form when a dreamer connects
them according to the laws of a chemistry uniquely his own, charging them with
all of the significations of a fate that can exist but once. There are dreams and
there are destinies: I am, above all, interested in the moment when destinies are
expressed through dreams.

---

* Much remains, however, to be said about dreams of levitation, not in terms of Freud, whose
narrowly sexual interpretation still strikes me as erroneous, but in regard to the levitation of the
mystics, Saint Teresa among others. In all of the dreams of levitation which I have experienced or
about which I have knowledge, the flight is always quite low, never above two or three meters.
There is never a soaring or ascension, but a sort of aerial gliding motion during which the sleeper
occasionally redescends to lightly touch ground before rising to *a certain height*. The absence of
gravity which characterizes levitation and the very strict spatial limitations in which it is practiced
seem nearly analogous to the miraculous levitation of mystics in the waking state. This parallel
merits a study undertaken without prejudice or credulity.

My goal is to present a certain number of texts, the exactness of which I can guarantee, and not to propound a new system of dream, for which I am absolutely unqualified. But in the interest of the pages to follow, it is perhaps necessary to indicate my state of mind in approaching the narration of this sequence of dreams. To my way of seeing (and it goes without saying that this vantage point is extremely personal), the experience of the dreamer is not without analogy to that of the poet, and one could compare the oneiric components in their unpolished state, with their endlessly multipliable symbolic resonances, to the vulgar or exalted rhymes ranged alongside the columns of a dictionary. The sleeper assembles images the way the poet assembles words: he makes use of them more or less felicitously to speak about himself to himself. Just as there are mutes, there are sleepers who do not dream; others dream badly, tritely, or by fits and starts: there are stuttering and verbose dreamers. Others, among whom it would be sheer ingratitude on my part not to count myself, sometimes receive the benefice of a beautiful dream, like those sorry poets whom chance occasionally grants the windfall of a verse that astonishes even them. Finally, there are perhaps sleepers of genius who dream with sublimity every night. If only we had at our disposal collections, museums of dreams, we could doubtlessly authenticate the existence of a Delacroix, a Leonardo da Vinci, or Watteau of the world of closed eyes.

To assert that the sleeper makes use of his dreams as a means of expression might seem to overly disregard the fatal aspect of dreams. The author of sublime dreams is as narrowly determined in his interior climate as the parsimonious housewife who dreams of chipped saucepans, but the higher one rises on the Jacob's ladder that humanity climbs and descends, the more are liberty and fatality resorbed in each other to form the indivisible whole that is a destiny. A writer, who for thirty years has scrutinized his own dreams with a lucid and emotive curiosity, once confided in me that he was at last able to escape the zone of nightmare thanks to his own efforts as a sleeper: the nightmares miscarried, ended well, no doubt because this man now possessed the power to hold external adversities in check, precisely the privilege of those beings who have a personal fate.*

The gift of dream, like the gift of second sight, has, however, nothing to do with innate liveliness of intelligence, and a man of exceptional genius may well be an imbecile in his dreams. On the other hand, certain mystical aspirations, certain renunciations, a certain dangerous atmosphere of pure suffering or pure solitude are favorable to the birth of hallucinated dreams, and I have observed in my own case that the percentage of incoherent and worthless dreams diminishes for someone who endeavors to set a barrier of serenity opposite the trivial misfortunes of daily life. Just as many claim that after the age of forty a person is responsible for his own face, and no doubt his destiny, it might likewise be said that maturity and old age are responsible for their dreams.

The dreams that compose this volume are all my own, and I have refused to allow myself to incorporate narration of the beautiful dreams that at times have been confided in me, on the one hand because I believe that it is impossible to manage describing with rigorous exactitude all of the minute details of a foreign dream, and on the other because it may interest the reader to know that all of the following dreams emanate from the same being, are the facets of one encompassing dream. But prefaces are made to receive the exceptions that would destroy a book's harmony. I insist on noting here the nightmare of an elderly woman, who saw herself once more in her childhood house, but in a reversed house, where the doors that opened to the right in her diurnal memories opened to the left in dream; and where the stairwell, the clock in the vestibule occupied

---

* This concerns Edmond Jaloux, thanks to whose encouragement this book was in part undertaken. Jaloux was often imprisoned, almost defeated by his daily life and even by his life as a novelist, which he seemed to live as heedlessly as his real life, often with the worse possible results; only his life as a critic was controlled and lucid, and this *is how he aspired to lead* his dreamed life. We often discussed the rift between dreams and reality. It was always he who at last underlined the difference; the dream is entirely *given* to us. So at ease with the books on which his criticism was brought to bear, perhaps he also considered these books written by others as given, while his life as a novelist (and he judged himself to be very mediocre), as well as his life in general, had to be revised each morning, just as it is for us all.

an exactly identical though exactly opposite place to that which had been assigned to them in life. But what matters in this instance is not the dismal impression emitted by this dream, but the curious example it affords of a dream about dream. A sublime Persian superstition would have it that for every arrival in the world of a human being there corresponds the birth of a creature belonging to the race of genies, which are reproduced only through the intermediary of man and are neither our guardians, nor our demons, nor our doubles in the occult sense of the word, but a sort of reflection cast upon the invisible. When a human child cries in its cradle, it is because his impalpable brother is pulling his hair; if he smiles in his sleep, it is because his fairy brother is telling him amusing tales. Sexual failures are explained by the jealousy of these insubstantial beings, who envy humans the privileges of love and it is in order to thwart their ambush that it is considered wise to leave a little light near newlyweds. Finally, when a man or woman dies, the nation of genies arrives to fetch the ethereal brother or sister and carries it away for burial in the empyrean. Whenever I ponder this belief that endows human life with the beauty of castles reflected in their moats, embellished by their tremulous image with a mystery they would otherwise lack, as if their reflection were reflected upon them, I tell myself that the impalpable landscapes of dream belong perhaps to this same fairy universe of reflections and mirages, of the mirror and the desert. We have not sufficiently observed that the symbols in books of popular oneiromancy are explained by their opposites, as if the compilers of the naive Dreambooks somehow suspected that it was also their task to interpret a world distorted or righted by a play of mirrors. The mirror corrects images, deforms, or reverses them: these three alternatives correspond to the three modes of dreams, whether a matter of beautiful dreams that restore an ideal radiance to reality, nightmares that return an image of our own life as grotesque as it is fearful, and fearful precisely because it is grotesque, or finally those dreams wherein the inverted symbols serve to dissemble secret and dangerous truths, just as the reversed script of Leonardo da Vinci helped preserve him from the scaffold. Every sleeper is a Narcissus who takes fright and is fulfilled above an eternal silvering, and the mind of the man who does not dream is neither more barren nor more confined than any other, but is, quite simply, like a room lacking that magic bay window of the mirror.

Another phenomenon, distinct from the play of mirrors, is allied to dream, and more specifically to a variety of dreams not yet mentioned: dreams of longing. This is the phenomenon of mirage in which it would seem that nature compensates, strives to create for its own eyes the illusion of groves in the steppe, a sheet of water in the desert. We have all of us never dreamed so abundantly as during our periods of longing, or of pain, which is but a wounded longing. And just as in a given place, a mirage does not change its aspect but repeats with the same humble and monotonous obstinacy the image of the shade that is lacking or of the pond for which nature thirsts, our dreams of longing revolve around a restricted number of themes, no more numerous and no more complicated than our misfortunes. The wardrobe of the dream of longing holds innumerable disguises, but only a small number of real personages hide behind the masks cut out from the very fabric of the night. As in Greek tragedy, the other silhouettes that cross the stage remain vague or summarily delineated, much like the confidants and messengers of Aeschylus. Similarly, the oneiric stage design, as sumptuous, as magnificent as it may be, is demonstrably less varied than the places where we have walked with open eyes. Many of us have wandered over a good portion of the world, have caressed many hands, have slept in more than one bed, have contemplated the countless masterpieces that diversify and enrich the idea that they form of beauty. But these superficial acquisitions[*] can only slightly influence the regimen of the soul itself, the muffled and slow life of the instinct that continues murmuring within us like a fountain, and we persist in dreaming of the few landscapes that recall those of our childhood, of the few churches similar to those in which our ancestors might have prayed, or

---

[*] Are they really superficial or are they set on a different, more elevated plane than that of dream, because closer to *lived reality*?

of the few beings whom we have lost or whom we need in order to assuage our suffering. In the even universe of sleep, these successive objects of our longing and our fear escape the division of space into compartments, the principle of contradiction that opposes being and becoming, the sectioning of the world by the clock-hand, rendering futile all conjecture whether a specific dream is formed of premonitions or reminiscences, since the gravitation of time, which is hardly anything but the form of our own weight, has no sway over these profoundly light images made from the same substance as our soul. Time exists because we sink perpendicularly into death, with feet closed together, dragged along by our millstone of flesh. But the images of our vampires and our angels float in this pure space where we plummet with vertiginous speed, without hope of return.

In the following pages, the disciple of Freud will encounter, in almost every line, images that are easy to translate according to his system of symbols, perhaps too easy. If these texts serve to confirm him in his theories, I will not complain, but it is not for this purpose that I have collected them, no more than with the opposite intent. Freudian theory easily finds an application in childhood dreams, considering the immense role that physiological processes and curiosity about them play at that period of existence; since mental illness perhaps represents a delay or regression to an early stage, the dreams of the disordered confess with the same cruel evidence as children's dreams. I mentioned earlier that, with one exception only, I do not remember a single lyrical dream that can be traced back to this period; on the other hand, I was often visited between the ages of seven and eight by the most banal of nightmares; in dreams, I saw a bloody and mutilated body fall into a room through the conduit of a singularly large, dark chimney. My sleeping little girl's reasoning explained this event by the presence upstairs of burglars, about whose exploits the maids often read aloud from the evening papers in my presence, but it now strikes me as plausible that this was actually a dream of giving birth, resulting from curiosity about sexuality, or rather about procreation, on the part of a little girl who must often have heard whispered allusions to her mother, deceased in childbirth, and to the use of

forceps at the moment of her birth. * *On the contrary, in those dreams that I
would readily characterize as domestic, composed of inconsiderable details of
daily life, the application of a symbolic key could well be superfluous, and when
a gardener dreams of a wheelbarrow, it is not untoward to suppose that a real
wheelbarrow might, on occasion, be intended. In the great* classic *or* magic
dreams *to which I alluded earlier, the Freudian interpretation satisfies without
completely convincing us: the dream of levitation may be of a sexual disposition,
as aforementioned; it may also be an ancient totemic dream of the assimilation
of man with bird; and the dreams of pursuit and exhibitionism possibly betray
an impulse to flee societal constraint or rebel against it, which would not,
however, exclude the presence therein of some degree of sexual symbolism.
Concerning the dream and almost everything else in the world besides, the most
apt explanations are arranged around the object for which they must account
somewhat in the manner of circles that readily spread out to infinity while always
remaining concentric to the object itself, at best encircling it more and more
narrowly, though unable to intersect its heart. The Freudian hypothesis provides
an almost satisfactory equation for the mystery of dreams; following different
pathways, the speculations of the occultists attained the same result, just as did
those of pharaoh's magi. Whatever the nomenclature, it is always the same
quantity that lies in the scale of the precision-balance. The problems of the mind
are by nature limitless; and those posed by the dream doubtlessly possess an
infinite number of solutions.*

*Whichever theory one chooses, one always concludes by ascertaining the
importance of a system of images which, if not perhaps presaging the sleeper's*

---

* At present, I doubt this Freudian interpretation and believe more in the influence of the
horrifying news items told with relish by the maids. In any case, if this childhood dream had to
do with my own birth, it would not contradict what I had elsewhere asserted about the healthy
indifference of a little girl for a mother deceased in childbirth, of whom she never heard
mentioned, but the detail of the forceps delivery, occasionally recollected in my proximity in
more or less hushed tones, could not help but interest a child passionately inquisitive, as are all,
about the physical process of labor.

future, does, in any case, reveal his present and past, and, furthermore, is most apt to predict the future to the extent that it acknowledges this present and past. In every epoch, the connoisseurs of oneiric matters have distinguished between dreams issuing from the gate of horn and dreams issuing from the gate of ivory; they have distinguished between useless and clumsy dreams that mean but little and those striking dreams that mean something, the same distinction evident between those actions to which chance and fatality compel a man and those which arise from his innermost being and compose the web of his personal destiny. If I were asked how exactly these lyrical or hallucinated *dreams are to be recognized, I would first mention a certain intensity of the colors, an impression of solemnity and mysterious rarefaction, into which enters something almost of terror and a hint of ecstasy, which only the word "awe" most nearly approximates. Then I would emphasize the inalterable character of this sort of dream: while the majority of dreams dissolve upon awakening in a mist of fatigue from which only a few inconsistent details emerge, the hallucinated dreams are cut out in sharp relief against the clear air of the night. As unmotivated and usually as deprived of conclusion as the others, they are characterized by an inner cohesiveness absent in the rest of dreams. It is impossible to change anything, to omit anything under pain of leaving a gaping rent or the mark of repair in the narration. With course set and fixed forever, they retain, over the years, the same monumental immobility by which are known the few great and moving memories of our life, which rarely coincide with the agitated and banal series of exterior events but which will doubtlessly be the only ones that we carry away to God.*

When I think about my life, I behold again a few strolls beside the sea, a nude little girl in front of a mirror, some scattered gusts of pitiful music in a hotel corridor, a bed, a few trains whose speed crushed the countryside, Venice at dawn, Amsterdam beneath the rain, Constantinople at sunset, the lilacs of the rue de la Varenne, someone dying, roaming the halls of a clinic in a fur-lined cloak, the red box of a theater, a young woman whose face turned all mauve because she was standing under a violet-colored lamp, the calcined hills of Greece, a field of daffodils in the countryside near Salzburg, a few dismal streets in the old northern towns where my sadness paced at set times before the shop fronts of corn chandlers or dealers in bootblacking, the grand basin at Versailles beneath a weighted sky of November, a camel stall filled with animals munching blood red melon, a parting near a subway entrance, a hand holding an anemone, the sweet sound of the blood in beloved arteries, and these few dozen lightning flashes are what I call my memories. These fragments of actual events have the magic intensity of the visions glimpsed in my dreams; and conversely, certain visions in my dreams have all the weight of events that have been lived through. Only my reason prevents me from confounding the two orders of phenomena, but this same reason counsels me to perhaps reconcile them, to place them, one beside the other, on a plane which is doubtlessly that of the sole reality.

Aside from a few older dreams, recognizable by the very brevity which made me choose to incorporate them in this complicated suite where they will appear in the state of pure tonalities, this entire series of dreams is set between the nights of my twenty-eighth and thirty-third year. All gravitate around a few same feelings, a few same signs. Only the advice of a friend[*] and the wish to bring additional evidence to bear in this so very obscure process of dream have induced me to remove them from the silence that covered them over like velvet. I feel reassured by thinking that these few meteoric stones fallen from my inner world will naturally have no more interest for others than mineralogical specimens arranged in a museum display case, and that their secret, talismanic warmth will continue to be perceptible only by me. Like everyone else, I have often considered someday writing a volume of intimate recollections: scruples, all too obvious to those of sound mind, dissuade me in advance from this venture which only the hardiest or perhaps the most hardened soul could undertake without lies. The publication of the ensuing narrations entails less glaring disadvantages, and this is what empowers me, facing myself, to bring to light these few episodes from the memoirs of my dreamed life.

M. Y.

---

[*] Edmond Jaloux is again in question.

The Visions in the Cathedral

I am standing in the transept of a church. Which church? A Gothic cathedral of gray rough stone, Chartres, Lausanne, perhaps Canterbury, a stone forest of full-grown trees, stripped of soaring birds and soaring angels, without ornamental brushwood rimed with silver or reddened with golden filaments, without hangings of waving tapestries, with nothing of the subdued magnificence of Saint Stephen's in Vienna, also with none of the crowding of corpses carved in marble, polished as the purest ivory, which transforms Westminster into a hangar hovering over the river Lethe. Upon the draughtboard of black and white flagstones, chairs are slovenly arranged, their angles marking the more or less abrupt way in which the devout arose at the end of a prayer to take their leave of God. A cathedral where, for the moment, no divine service is being celebrated, a cathedral without music, without incense, without candles, but also without asphyxiating darkness, a cathedral bathed in a clear penumbra which seems to trickle from the stones and slowly augments in the distance of the perspectives. I am not sure if I am the only visitor to this cathedral, or if prayers rise in the shadows or embraces are exchanged there; I observe no signs. A cathedral that appears to be empty; a cathedral at twilight; a cathedral on an ashen day.

An elderly woman draws near to me: this is a woman renting chairs. She is also an American, a certain Mrs. Knife, an old withered American woman battered by life, whom I had met in a Belgian hotel, flanked by her tubercular husband and syphilitic son, and whom I usually avoid because her dull chatter only deals with the comings and goings of duchesses, and because it is distressing to be unpleasant with people whom you pity. Here, she is far from her husband and son and she does not speak. She is just ridiculous enough to be touching and she no doubt resembles at this moment all that is best in her soul. She wears a bandage over her left eye, for she is threatened with going blind, and her right eye is all red, as if she no longer used it except for weeping. She approaches a prayer stool, before which I had stopped by chance, and I notice that a large satchel is propped against the small bars of the back. This seems to be one of those large, black leather portfolios in which print dealers shut up their collections and from which they draw out, one after another beneath the client's gaze, the inevitable portraits of Beethoven, the slender, half-nude young women destined to decorate the walls of bachelor's rooms, and the forever artificially blue seascapes. The American with her countenance of an unfortunate Fate hurries to untie the ribbons of the satchel and the pictures it contains flow beneath my gaze, one after the other, without my knowing how she makes them file before me. I have the impression that the image from underneath emerges to the surface at the right moment and is superposed by itself over the preceding image, without confusion, without a jolt, somewhat in the manner of those broad prospects that fill a screen during a film projection, and it is as if corners of countryside, of rooms, of celestial space were suddenly introduced into the twilight cathedral. Much more than painted landscapes, these are immobilized landscapes; the air bathes them but does not circulate there. You would say that a very gentle spell cast over them has put a stop to their changing. I know beyond question that these magic surfaces were painted by the man whom I loved and were, for some reason or other, placed there by him long ago. I even believe that he had painted them for no one but me, surely not that he had destined them for me, but because we have indefensible claims to rejoice in those things we were born to love and these abstract rights are the only ones that can never again be taken from us. It was foreordained that I would one day enter this church, that this satchel would be placed against this chair, and that an old Mrs. Knife whom I barely know would show me these canvases where the hands which were the dearest in the world to me had fixed images as vast as the earth and sky.

First, there is a staircase. A simple, white marble staircase with a banister supported by a row of balusters, lost in the midst of a sloping meadow. But this meadow is not green; it is mauve, or rather, violet, for the grass has been overgrown and replaced by the meadow-saffron of autumn. The staircase seems to lead nowhere; perhaps it joins the two terraces of a park. The bottom of the stair vanishes into the mauve abundance; the upper part of the bank hides the sky, but it must be the close of day, the moment when the eyes of twilight are going to shut. The stairs, a little slanting, a little worn, are stained with a sort of moldiness, and veins meander in the depths of the indefinably white stone, of that white which hesitates between yellow and gray, and which only belongs to marble often exposed to the rain and sometimes to the sun, and to the discolored faces of the ill when they begin their decline. Each slender flower on its stem has a special look which distinguishes it from the crowd of its companions, like a beloved woman whom one would recognize in the midst of a multitude, but the general effect is of a single continuous sheet a single immense slant of mauve velvet, rich and soft as a fabric mellowed with age. But what I cannot express in words is the silent, delicate charm of this corner of a landscape, its compromise between sadness and serenity, the sense, diffused everywhere, of an intense expectation which is already no longer hope. As always in the presence of the lovely, peaceful aspects of the world, you have the impression that their very stillness is the result of a tragic tension and must end in annihilation. And perhaps it is that which endows this park where nothing happens with such poignancy, unless it is the sensation of day's end or the presence of flowers which only bloom in autumn.

The second image represents a young woman arrayed in a gown the color of wine dregs, standing out in relief against somber wainscoting of polished oak wood. You observe her to the waist, as if she were staying on the other side of an opened window. Her slightly distended leanness begets thoughts of Holy Virgins by Flemish primitives; her gentle, equine face is pierced by immense somber eyes, encircled as if she had wept black tears; her thin dark hair is pulled back from her forehead in Chinese fashion; her gourd-shaped breast gives suck to a nursling whose completely nude body is almost sienna. She looks straight ahead with a patience beyond resignation; if there is in the depths of her being a hint of frightened sadness, she must be the first to be unaware of it; and her large bony hands are as serene as her eyes.

Afterwards, there is an expanse of level grassland discovered from a bird's-eye view, a vast pale green plain, of the touching green of growing grass, and the millions of timid blades that pierce the epidermis of the earth are as soft as the down on the poorly closed skull of a newborn child. The purity of the atmosphere is so perfect that you can see the grass growing from above, as you might, in the purest silence, hear it increase. This broad expanse of green, flown over from a very great height, recalls the fleeting hue of certain racecourses, or the acid pallor which the burnt hills of the south assume in March when they strive to make us believe that they, too, enjoy a springtime.

Then there is a woman standing in the midst of the void, her feet alighted on space. I notice nothing of her face except a sort of white orb. She is clothed in heavy draperies of rich, dense blue, which vibrate against the blue black ground of the sky. Scattered bronze clouds resembling monsters, fabrics, birds float in the ether. Two winged creatures have knelt on those clouds at the feet of that strange, zodiacal goddess: their angular attitudes and their clothing that writhes and unfolds behind them conjure reveries of the chimerical jinn of the Far East rather than of angels, and their very bodies and hair also resemble lacerated silk stuff, clouds, solar animals, Medusae from the depths above.

Lastly, there is a stained glass window. For this final image is not set down against the back of the prayer stool: it hovers strangely above the satchel, at the place where the wall of the transept is often pierced by a rose window. A tree of Jesse stripped by winter, its roots and branches growing round symmetrically, delineates an orb which is the circumference of this blue rose window. The trunk, the boughs, the deep tentacles are Prussian blue, of that almost black blue of the Atlantic on a day of high wind and of human arteries full of blood and salt. Roots and twigs bathe in the sky, drink the sky, transform it into sap. And in this sky of liquid sapphire, rays of a scorching coldness throb like the blue beacon of Sirius during the longest nights of the year.

At the moment when Mrs. Knife approaches for the sake of tying the ribbons of the satchel again, bundled letters fall from between the sheets of blotting paper and scatter on the ground: a packet of envelopes checkered with stamps from all points of origin, some empty and others with the sheets of writing paper they contained reinserted between their carelessly opened edges. All of these envelopes bear one and the same name, one and the same address. I do not remember the syllables which compose that name, and since I had no feeling of having forgotten something upon awakening, it is probable that I had also not spelled them out in the dream. But I know, in some mysterious way, that this is the name of the man I loved, his true name, the one that he does not bear in life, and of which I was unaware until this day. The discovery of this name fills me with a magic happiness and confidence more pure than the rabbi's to whom the possession of four ineffable vowels suddenly confers an advantage of God.

"Ah," I say, "at last, I know your true name."

And my own cry of joy awakens me, altogether bathed in voluptuousness.

The Accursed Pond

This ill-favored dream dates back to the nights of my childhood: it is the very oldest, most suffocating and most northerly of my nightmares. An unassuming meadow in the shape of an almost perfectly rounded basin with a small pool, the color of lead, outstretched in its hollow. Wild oats, wild celery, all sorts of malignant and undisciplined plants thrive in the damp weeds and a few stunted trees grow aslant in the sloping earth. A westerly wind, that soft, moist, slightly salt-tinged wind that bears the rain in northern lands, blows close to the ground and sorrowfully sweeps over the weeds which tremble and display their gray reverse. Dirty white reflections swiftly skim the pond and resemble the irksome, flashing light of metal flags placed in the crook of fruit trees to warn away birds. The low weighted sky seems formed of an accumulation of still smoke. Some wild poppies, a scattering of huge, red flower cups, blaze now and then in the gray weeds and alone ignite this corner of leaden earth which they seem to stain with blood. These flowers redolent with the juice of sleep and death, this pallid lake which seems forever poisoned by a spell cast into its very heart, are more familiar to me than many landscapes where I have walked some twenty times in broad daylight. And even though this dream has returned to me only at rare intervals, I have the feeling of having spent very few nights without once again beholding this place which bears for me the stamp of a desolation far less assuring than the loneliness of graveyards. A few years ago in Zeeland in the countryside near Middelbourg, I recognized the same incessant trembling of the grass in the insipid sea breeze that I must often have observed during my childhood, on the Flemish hills between Lille and the sea, and which, no doubt, was imparted to my dreams. And as for the little pond, ill-omened of aspect, I have not yet encountered it while awake, but I know that on the day that I find it, I must interpret its presence as an incitement to commit suicide.

The most evolved versions of this dream do not allow any human character, but one does see a few familiar objects scattered about as in designs for a puzzle. There lies a pair of old shoes, down at the heel, half hidden in the thick grass, or a cracked copper pail once used by milkmaids for their evening task, some dung on which you step and which splits with a harsh sound, a worm-eaten stool on which I sit but which collapses beneath my weight and this incident, humorous and insipid, flings me out of my dream. At last, in a more tragic epilogue in which this dream veers to nightmare, a huge she-cat, dirty rust in color, is snatched from the crook of a tree beneath which I am seated. I recognize her: it is the gardener's cat, turned wild again after her young had been taken from her to be drowned in the pond and my brother had to destroy it with a gunshot. The shot goes off without a sound; once again the shot strikes the huge shaggy body; the dreadful phosphorescent pupils pitch back and are extinguished; the body, with belly still distended from recently birthing its litter, falls with a thudding, slightly repulsive noise, curls up, and finally disappears beneath the grass. The high clover leaves, which reach to my shins, close over the dead animal and I see nothing more, spreading over a large fern indolently swayed, than a long and clammy trail of blood.

The Pathway beneath the Snow

I am moving forward through a snow-covered plain that appears boundless to me beneath a gray sky from which all of this whiteness has descended. In the air, not a breath. All sensations of cold, of weariness, of dangerous isolation in the midst of space without shelter are excluded from the start of this dream: nothing within it recalls the exhilarating effort of long wintry walks, the bright song of the blood, the facial skin cut as if by the edges of a crystal. Neither does anything here suggest the exhausting struggle, related to nightmare, of wresting with every step one's soles from the yielding white mass. I advance effortlessly upon a ground of firmly packed snow that chinks and cracks beneath my steps; my solitude is not anxious and the immensity is not hostile. So much serenity, so much silence call to mind the apt English expression "still life," designating not deathly inanimation but Being in a state of repose. It is only in the final measures of this dream that a shiver of physical cold succeeds in stealing into me, but this entire prelude is of an immaculate calm.

The heavy snow unfurls its peaceful undulations in all directions, covering over what yesterday must still have been ditches, hedges, all of the irregular ground of the fields. You sense, beneath the white layer, the presence of the two deep, beaten tracks of the roadway, which stretch out as far as the eye can reach between two slightly swollen embankments that hem the edge of this long sinuous ribbon set flat against the snow, and scarcely more visible in all of this white than a vanishing wake upon a tranquil sea. On the horizon, at the spot where the sky weighs against the earth, the gray sky becomes a black sky.

At one of the bends in the road, approaching me from afar, I see an affable and commanding walker fitted with red boots that hasten with a long undisturbed stride. One would say a white snowball, perhaps tinged with pink, set upon two long vermilion-colored stilts. This is a stork or a flamingo, the animal of Islam and of Christmas, the one that conveys the newborn through northern skies and in the Orient perches on the domes of tombs. In passing close to me, she graciously extends her foot and shakes my hand for a moment.

After a few steps, at a second bend in the road, I encounter another bird, this time a falcon that is dead or perhaps stiffened with cold, an animal with glazed eyes lying in the snow. I gather him up tenderly. I place him in my bosom with the hope of warming him against my blood and, indeed, the proud animal soon revives, stirs about, and finally comes to perch on my shoulder.

I am conscious of a bond that nothing can break, of a friendship that will never end, of a certainty that excludes all suspicion and fear and can even withstand the risks of separation, as if I were sure that the well-beloved bird of prey would always come back in the end to perch against my cheek. But a fresh bend in the road appears: we pass in front of a little farm, buried in snow, an unassuming, little one-story cottage with a farmyard entirely trellised with brass wire, after the manner of a large birdcage, and where the only domestic animals are, indeed, birds. While leaning my face against the flexible lozenges of the trellis, I observe that the irregularities and hollows in the old wall closing the back of the yard serve as roosts and shelters for hundreds of birds that have established their broods here, as if it were nesting season. Tits, bullfinches, goldfinches pass their heads with lively eyes through the round cavities in the wall, profusely draped with four-o'clocks and passionflowers that seem unaware of the proximity of the snow, almost as when during nocturnal crossings through the channel of Corinth, the thousands of falcons, nestled inside the holes left by dynamite in the trench of the isthmus, protrude their heads and fasten their mesmerized pupils on the slow reflections of the packet-boat beacons projected on the two bare stone walls. Without my being able to explain how he managed to get through the metal fence, I suddenly see my falcon on the other side of the grating in the midst of the broods of defenseless birds. At first, I expect a massacre of the innocents, but nothing of the sort occurs, and the celestial bird of prey appears to live in good fellowship with the bullfinches and goldfinches. With heart reassured about the songbirds' fate, I resume my path without heeding his desertion.

The third station is a pit dug from the snow, surrounded by almost-consumed candles burning close to the ground. The road leads to this pit. There is nothing beyond but a thick wall of snow made from the excavation of that soft and soothing white tomb. Despite its depth, I descend easily into the pit and I lie down there, for I am sleepy. But at the end of a long space of time, which I cannot measure with any precision, I begin to feel cold. I realize that it would be best to get up from this glacial bed and resume the same road in the opposite direction. Besides, the wall of snow prevents me from venturing to the other side of my tomb. I've hardly gone a few steps when the falcon from which I was just separated returns to alight on my shoulder, and I seek the homeward path with this animal of the resurrection as my companion for the roadway.

Torn-out Hearts

A kitchen, a sink near the window, a table covered with oilcloth, checkered in white and blue. On that table, a woven basket brimming with red and slimy things resembling the entrails of recently drawn chickens and into which I am forced to plunge my hands. I know that these are hearts, nothing but hearts, hearts of men and women, with bits of arteries and filaments of poorly removed veins. But I do not know which living persons these hearts belonged to. They persist in beating with the unendurable din of watches hanging in a clockmaker's display, and the entire kitchen resounds with their insistent and conflicting ticktock, mocking the servant girl's alarm. You can see them in the basket heaped on top of each other, by turns expanding and contracting with the horrible jolts that distinguish the death throes of suffocating fish. I tell myself that one way or another they must be forced into stillness, on pain of not hearing the bell sound in the hallway and the footsteps of the employee from the Galeries Lafayette coming to deliver the Christmas tree; and, in vain, I smother five or six damp rags on top of the container which continues to stir like a rush basket full of vipers. Finally, to get rid of that noise that will make me scream in the end, I very carefully pour the basket's viscous contents out of the open window between the hands, joined and hollowed like a shell, of a young beggar with a face lit up by sunburn, who is waiting down below between the backstairs and the trench of the garage and who wears around his brown neck the pale and threadbare ghost of a blue kerchief.

The Corpse in the Ravine

I am incarcerated in a prison dug into the summit of a colossal crag, hewn out of the stone by unskilled laborers who have left the trace of hammer and pickax in the uneven granite. The dark cell is lit only by an air trap provided with iron bars that intersect at equal angles and form large crosses; it opens directly upon the blue and vacant sky, where not even the birds venture; you do not see the sun and the light does not enter through the black hole, but the calm and, as it were, rested azure of the beautiful summer's afternoon is inalterably resplendent behind the hard small bars. The cell holds nothing but an empty pitcher, and a heap of blond straw shines in the most distant corner of my prison. Two nude little children with very dark skin gambol and gently roll on the straw that crumples with a fresh sound. Each wears nothing but a large bracelet, perhaps the last link of their shackles; sweat gleams on their plump bodies, deeper and more burnished than the most beautiful bronze; they are not sad; they seem completely unaware of my presence; and tangled together, they nibble and lick each other, belabor each other with friendly blows like two puppies from the same litter.

I am standing in front of the vent, with hands clutching the bars. If I raise myself on tiptoe, I discover, on the other side of the ravine, the summit of large jagged rocks that stand out in profile against the blue sky like long flames metamorphosed into stone. The boulder where my rock-cut prison has been hollowed seems to belong to an entirely closed amphitheater of mountains, and the narrow, deep abyss that opens in the middle is no larger than those airless courtyards where the windows of kitchens and maid's rooms receive the daylight in the hidden part of grand buildings. The sides, corroded, charred, the color of lions and furnaces, descend perpendicularly to the bottom of this chasm that forms a sort of prison beneath the open sky, and no crevice, no cavern's mouth fissures their vertical, slick extent. In cautiously passing my head between the bars, I can see, all the way at the bottom, the ground strewn with rocks. I know that it is in this trench that Greek prisoners condemned to death had been massed; they had just been led away to be all the more efficiently massacred on the plain; only one remains behind, a wounded man, already so mortally struck that they have disdained to put him to death. This young man comes and goes, crawling on the ground of his deep cage of savage rocks, feeling the rough walls with his hands as if blinded by glaring reflections from the rock and from distress, and, everywhere, he knocks his head against the vertiginous bulk of stones. From time to time, he manages to lift himself alongside the rock to a height of a spear's length or two, then falls again, and each time yet another contusion is added to his wounds. By dint of shaking the bars of my prison, I manage to pull them away from their fastenings; they remain in my hands like black and blighted teeth out of a gaping mouth. But I lean forward in vain, and the opening of the air trap is far too narrow for my entire body to go through.

Then a tall woman, gaunt and forbidding, clothed in a long yellow dress that delineates the muscles of her flat chest, makes her entrance into my prison; she is unquestionably the jailer. With a nod, she compels me to follow her, and I find myself before a doorway that I had not suspected. The key that I am handed enables me to work the lock soundlessly, and we find ourselves on a sort of terrace, scarcely a few cubits wide, bordered with pointed rocks with the appearance of crenels. The woman gestures toward a narrow staircase with steps almost effaced with wear that spirals between the fallen rocks and descends to the extremity of the ravine. The low doorway closes behind me, and, in solitude, I must attempt my climb down the length of this skeletal staircase, unused, it would seem, for centuries except by red ants. The steps are so high, so slippery, not even steps but blocks of stone set one on top of the other, that I succeed in descending only at the cost of strenuous effort, and I must set my bare feet down with extreme care to avoid repulsive contact with the giant ants. Among the red rocks, the air is a blue rock, as dense, as hard as the other stones. The void that surrounds me conveys so completely the impression of a solid surface that I feel not the slightest dizziness but only the perilous desire to set my heel on that smooth flagstone which seems to extend the rock. Little by little, as I gradually force my way down, the sky above me loses something of its brightness, turns pale before darkening for the night. We have reached the moment of solemn armistice between the darkness and the blue, between the sun and the stars. A remainder of day is concentrated at the bottom of the ravine, as is a little water in the hollow of a valley during times of drought. I understand that the sun is in the act of setting somewhere behind the mountains, but I do not know on which side the *west* is to be found. The silence in the ravine is extraordinary, inhuman, almost suffocating, for no breeze arrives to freshen it, and the wall of rocks checks the silken sound of the wind. A last step, more precipitous than the others, compels me to go down in a seated posture, helping myself along with palms and loins. When I arrive level with the ground, the young soldier is already dead.

He has just died, for his body has still not acquired the rigidity that distinguishes corpses, and his broken limbs preserve a kind of living softness. He is outstretched on a slab of rock striped with deep fissures, with his head dragged by the weight of his helmet to hang almost level with the ground. In the hollow of his helmet of burnished metal, where the black curls of his hair abound like dark foam, I can observe nothing of his face but the deep, blue bruises beneath his closed eyelids and the beautiful, slightly swollen mouth that his bronze chin strap keeps closed in spite of death. He is completely nude: his chest grows hollow, emptied of breathable air, crushed by the tremendous mass of the blue sky that nothing inside his partially deflated lungs can ever again resist; his sex rests between his thighs with the innocence of a sleeping child; his legs, tightly welded together, possess the majesty of overturned columns; and a lone sandal remains suspended from one of his feet, where the nails have begun to turn blue. His bare arms trail from both sides of his bed of stone, lightly touching the ground with their slightly swollen fingers that seem to trace an incomprehensible sign in the dust. His blood, which streams from a gaping wound in his left thigh, flows away into the ravine and is mingled with the gathering darkness; and his entire body is flecked with countless little bruises, mauve or violet, streaked with imperceptible white veins. Upon closer inspection, I discover that what I had taken for bruises are as many moths glued to this corpse, sucking his blood with the help of their long, mosquitoes' antennae. The thousand gorged monsters rustle while weakly stirring their transparent wings, then indolently take flight above the corpse and whirl round in the twilight.

The Keys to the Church

I walk alongside a canal where lifeless branches are floating past. Before me, a stone's throw distant, a man and a woman advance indolently while conversing in a hushed whisper. The woman is one of my friends of former times, dead now for many years but whose death I learned of only long months after having this dream; the man is still alive, but at this moment, within my dream, they are both equally alive or equally deceased. It is the end of a rainy afternoon: pale glimmers are reflected in puddles of water. Suddenly, the quay's sharp turnings put us face to face with a Gothic cathedral in gray stone; this cathedral is partially concealed by the swarm of tottering hovels that lean against its sides, so that one can only really make out the upper part of the smooth, unadorned facade, pierced by a rose window that seems a somber diamond from the outside, and its gigantic buttresses, set off in relief against the dusk and recalling the vertebrae of some immense dead animal. Beneath the low sky, the houses on all sides of the square bow their great uneven roofs of steep incline where trails of glistening raindrops continue to glide here and there. The man and woman who go before me continue to advance without interrupting their mysterious, whispered confidences; they are both wearing dark gray clothes of commonplace and slightly outmoded cut. Finally, with slow and supple step, the woman precedes her companion and resolutely enters into the church through the half-open door of the great portal, its leaf closing by itself behind her.

I have drawn closer to the man in the gray suit, who has made me a hasty bow just as if we had taken leave of each other the day before. Both of us strive in vain to move the heavy bronze lock: someone explains to us that this is the closing hour for churches and that we need to address the sacristan if we wish to enter. Accompanied by my father, who has also happened to join us, we are directed the length of a little street that follows the curves of the edifice toward the sacristan's lodge, where an old woman, kneeling beside a hearth, is roasting something over a wood fire. She explains to us that her husband is away and will not be back for an hour, and she offers to let us wait for him in front of the fire. But we prefer to avail ourselves of the fading light for the sake of strolling the quay, and, at last, we find an old worm-eaten bench where all three of us are finally seated in the presence of the flowing water.

Unknown to us, the sky, grayish until now, has by degrees become imbued with a miraculous rose color. The entire horizon recalls the faltering and yet intense nuance of rosé wine, or of a miraculous consecrated wafer preparing to bleed. The leaden river has chosen this same rose tinge and the difference between the sky and the water is not a difference of hue but rather of substance, like that which exists between watered silk and velvet. On the other side of the river, where but a moment ago only a heap of gray structures loomed, the eye now discovers an infinite shore, touched with the same mesmerizing rose color, and this almost flat expanse ascends in imperceptible modulations up to a hill that dominates the river and is covered with a strange agglomeration of ethereal buildings, as rose-colored as the sky. Ramparts, palaces, temples, latticed galleries, towers, and still more ramparts stand out against limitless space and, in this autumnal city that calls to mind Bruges or a mist-laden Haarlem, these palaces rising leisurely tier upon tier suddenly emerge like a kind of Hradisch or Kremlin of exalted delicacy, and are such as might only be glimpsed in dreams or in the hallucinated canvases of old masters.

A few steps from me on the quay, I see an old kneeling Levantine merchant, who is unpacking his small stock of goods. The carpets that his long hands spread out on the ground with a precise and somewhat caressing gesture are rose-colored, ineffably rose-colored like the landscape, the river, and the sky. In drawing closer to him, I note with astonishment that his gaunt brown face, the worse for wear rather than aged, resembles my own almost feature for feature, despite his expression of servility and cunning that I have never encountered in my mirror. The merchant, arrived from the islands of the Archipelago, explains to me in a failing voice broken with heart disease that he has landed in this city with the hope of finding his son, for his son had died in Venice. But his tale remains confused, and I do not believe that we are in Venice since I do not recognize the palaces and Venice was not built alongside a river.

Then, the Levantine merchant offers in the same low voice, a little lisping, seemingly made to convey obscene proposals to the ear, to help me find the sacristan's lodge since he must be back by now. While passing in front of the old bench where I was seated a few moments ago, I notice that my two former companions are no longer there; no doubt, they have gone before me into the church. I take my leave of the Levantine merchant whose presence has become useless to me now that the two men are inside the church and can open the door for me, and I am sure that I can find the way again to the great portal on my own.

But I didn't count on the growing darkness or on the thousand circuitous meanders of the narrow streets that circumvent the church. Lost in this labyrinth of small low houses overhung by the buttresses of the church that loom like a cliff above a fishing village, I do not succeed in finding the great portal again; the rare little doors, concealed at the bottom of the walls and discovered only in groping about blindly, are closed with shabby wooden leaves pierced with diminutive dormer windows, like those of old shops, and malignant candle glimmers wink behind the lozenges. When finally a band of pale whitish sky informs me that I am approaching the great empty expanse of the square where the outer sanctuary of the church opens, a young gypsy girl rushes down, jostles me, passes me, stations herself opposite me in the black narrow street, touching with her two hands the two walls of the ruinous houses, and barring my passage with her two arms held crosswise. Her body, half-nude under her rags, is as frail and emaciated as a martyr's; her tanned adolescent arms are of a slender and charming roundness, but they are gashed with bloody scratches, scattered with contusions. If the face of the aged merchant from a moment ago bore an older brother's resemblance, the terra cotta features of this savage little beggar resemble mine like a younger sister's. With her head slightly thrown back and teeth clenched, she stares at me with a look of anxious defiance which I know only too well, although I had never detected it in my own mirror, and soon I see, from very close up, nothing but her eyes, her blue eyes, her immense eyes, her marvelous eyes that belong to someone else.

The Blue Water

This is scarcely a dream: this vision all of a piece, all of one color, evades all nocturnal conventions; no plot, no scene-shifting, no characters, no vicissitudes, none of the stagecraft of a dream. Inert, asleep, I feel myself sinking in the pure depths of a blue ocean, fluid as the air of a spring morning, transparent as the clearest crystal, and the words "aquamarine" and "sapphire" are opaque and heavy compared to these precious, liquid layers, where the slightest movement, the mere weight of my body sustaining its balance between two depths, conveys a sweet, cool pressure. Without suffocating, I breathe in this water, transparent as the void and the sky, and this bliss, which cannot be expressed in language, would have to be translated here by a series of blue arpeggios. This limpid, physical joy might only be compared to that of a swimmer who plunges into the Blue Grotto in Capri at the height of a summer day. Such an immaculate chill precludes even the slightest hint of sexual symbolism, and yet, the perfect happiness, the unadulterated joy of this dream, prolonged after awakening just as the benefits of a swim remain with you throughout the sultry hours, evoke the beatific vision of love. It has happened to me often enough, namely three or four times in my life, to come out of a dream with restored serenity, refreshed, reassured, but the reasons for this delightful state are forgotten upon awakening, just as it has happened to all of us to suddenly come out of a nightmare, terrified by our own screams, but without the slightest memory of the danger that made us scream. Only this one dream, dreamt besides at a moment of intense physical exhaustion, bequeaths me an image, a symbol, the tremulous reflection of that salutary blue basin.

The unique character of this dream is perhaps attributable to a certain sensation of levitation in the water, which effortlessly yields and is opened, just as space in dreams of aerial levitation is opened and yields before the soaring of the winged sleeper. Gradually, as I climb again toward the surface and toward awakening, no doubt assimilated here with the surface of the world of dreams, I rend zones of a blue more and more light-saturated, almost impossible to distinguish from the sky. Everything is blue, of a dense blue but transparent, as if the perfect blue of the glass beads of Mytilene flowed away in dew. But the perfect sensation of the sea endures, the icy cold happiness relished in the depths of submerged caverns, which are perhaps nothing but the transposition of the most secret layers of the soul, where human balance is continuously recovered, where tears, blood, the flow of sap, the increase of hair, and the flowering of smiles are no doubt obedient to laws as reassuring as those of the surge and the stars. Finally, I float to the surface like a swimmer on his back, with eyes still closed but ready to open upon the white dome of the sky or upon the ceiling of my bedroom, when a large marine animal, sprung from the depths, approaches me, fidgeting its welcome in a joyous splash of blue water. It is an enormous seal, smooth and shiny as a rubber toy; the inside of his mouth is as clean and pink as the gums of infants, and he sniffles, caressing my face with his mild, healthy animal's breath. Planted against my chest, pressing against my shoulders with all the weight of both of his webbed paws, he pushes his snout provided with long mustaches toward my face and proceeds to lick my mouth, nose, cheeks with all the conscientious tenderness of a faithful dog. At that moment, also the moment of awakening, I turn my head imperceptibly and realize that this is indeed a faithful dog, the family dog, standing against the bed where I had thrown myself to fall into a brutish sleep after the exhaustion of a long journey, who embraces me with its rough tongue amidst joyful little yelps.

The Island of the Dragons

I am living with a young man and a young woman in the most confined of Venetian lodgings. Our room is located under the roofs, on the top floor of a complicated house that dominates from on high a rose and russet confusion of terraces, masts, campaniles, lean homeless cats and swallows' nests. Our single room is furnished with only a scattering of woolen carpets woven in Central Asia and dyed in beautiful hieratic colors, carpets of typically rough, tight nap, irritating to the touch and still permeated with the sweat of pack mules. There is also a set of aluminum cookware and a heap of cumbersome and luxurious English suitcases with locks that never manage to work. In the middle of the room, a uniformly red Dalmatian trunk holds a series of boxes made from old books emptied of their contents, like those sold in Paris by deluxe confectioners and dealers in knickknacks, inside which all of the species of seeds—sunflower, cumin, and anise—and all of the different sorts of bird feathers have been carefully classified. The young man and young girl spend the day arguing or making love on the carpets without taking off their heavy clothing, and my principal task is to continually readjust the Venetian blind that rattles and allows dust and irritating rays of sunlight to enter the room.

But the room in which we are living is decidedly too small; in the evening, in the darkness, we collide against the corners of the furniture, and, from fear of falling, we grasp the wallpaper that gives way and crumbles on us. The girl has decided to move: since we appear unconcerned about the choice of a new lodging, I assume that it has already been prepared for our arrival. The young man leaves, wearing a strange traveling suit of very pale green plaid, and is off in quest of a furniture mover and a barge. His companion, kneeling in front of the open suitcases, tosses in pell-mell all of the objects littering the floor of the room: neckties and books, alarm clocks and revolvers, a gorgeous collection of pink nightgowns, and sumptuous blankets, which softly offer resistance, form thick pads that overflow the lid of the suitcase, catching their fringes in the locks. Finally, by dint of bearing down with knees and fists on these rebellious suitcases, we manage to carefully lock them; we also close the Dalmatian trunk that remains practically empty; but the pots and pans haven't found a place anywhere, and the young girl throws them from the window into the barge, where they pile up with a crash. With the help of the young man, who has returned to the room in the nick of time, we lift the trunk and the suitcases to the window ledge: they follow the same aerial path. Then it is our turn, scorning door and staircase, to go down the void. Since we are holding each other's hands, we are sure of not falling. The air sustains us softly and yields underfoot like the tightrope that acrobats tread; at last, our own gravity draws us and gently sets us down in the already overladen barge that swings and sinks level with the flat, shining water. To move more freely in case of shipwreck, I've put on a sort of sailor's suit in black wool.

The moment I lay hold of the rudder, everything is transformed. The high, delicate houses that lined the canal disappear; I no longer see their somewhat oblique rose walls, like boat sails that yield to the slightest vibration of the wind. The posts used for the mooring of gondolas are still visible, but they resemble the leaning masts of boats already engulfed by the sea. The surface of the canal loses the pale and equivocal aspect of water tamed within city walls; we are sailing on a bracing, deep, green black density, its intense color apparently sustained and nourished by the very depths of the sea. A thick fog rises around us, hiding the limits of the wan horizon, even stifling the immense plashing of the roused sea against the sides of our barge. We are on the high seas, adrift in boundless space without assistance: we eagerly drink in this violet haze through all of the pores of our lips. Our boat without sails, without oars, without a motor advances with a gentle motion through this noiseless wadding. Seated in front, propped against her companion's shoulder, the young woman quietly pours forth tears as sorrowful as the ocean. A pile of luggage reels and is engulfed without a sound. Suddenly, a soft jolt informs us that our barge has landed; two slippery steps lead us to a sort of crenelated platform: we are in the outer court of a fortified castle, closely wed to the irregular contour of the islet on which it is built, its isolated mass washed on all sides by the ocean. The courtyard is deserted; the fortress seems to be empty. The barge strays imperceptibly from the landing place and sways very close to shore, at a trifling distance where we will never again be able to reach it. The young woman sits down with her back against the crenels and continues to be absorbed in her tears; the young man holds her hand; he is motionless, as if in the depths of a profound meditation, and his back is slightly bent beneath the weight of his thought.

A large low doorway with a rounded vaulted roof like the porch of a Romanesque church can be descried at no great distance from us, but the fog makes it look further away than it in fact is, and a few steps of white stone raise it above the gray pavement of the courtyard. Gradually, we discover that this hermetically sealed doorway is no common threshold; it seems that its door-leaves are made of loadstone and that my companions' garments must be charged with iron filings. An indefinable force draws them to that closed doorway, and yet, they are afraid; a vague and calm fear, diffuse as the anguish of someone who is sickening with a grave illness, gently stirs their vital organs but does not penetrate their conscious thought. Apparently still unaware of danger, they are thus robbed of all ability to contrive some means of defense necessary for their salvation. They have the look of being at once numb and uneasy, and their walk, interrupted with abrupt stops, is reminiscent of the pace of sleepwalkers and spellbound birds. Hand in hand, they approach that doorway behind which must swarm tremendous and deformed creatures, more repulsive than dreadful, resembling, all at once, serpents, bats, and caterpillars. They finally come to a stop two steps away from the threshold: after long waiting, the door soundlessly parts a crack, as silently as a velvet curtain is lifted; and the young woman vanishes into that chink scarcely wide enough to afford a passageway for her body. A few minutes later, the young man in plaid clothing is swallowed up in turn; and the indolent mist, the weighted silence, forms once again around the sealed doorway. I know that it will never again reopen, and I am not afraid. But I also know that I am alone, on an islet without hope, lost in the moaning immensity of the sea.

The waves rise insensibly, lapping the crenels on the wall and gradually covering over the platform where I am seated. They lift me: I abandon myself to their infinite rocking. I experience no anguish; on the contrary, the balancing of the mild surge is full of sweetness. The barge has long been submerged in the depths of the sea; only the Dalmatian trunk still emerges. I set my hands on it, as if on a life buoy, but it soon transforms into a simple basket of red straw in which an infant lies sleeping like Moses on the waters. The basket sinks in turn: only my body and this frail infant are unsinkable, and I float, folded in on myself, reclosed over this warm little flesh like the myriad spirals of a shell, while the newborn's hair grows with miraculous speed, lengthens beyond all measure, twines around my arms, my legs, my nude torso, and flows here and there in undulations like roots of seaweed.

The Avenue of the Beheaded

I am strolling with my father in the Esterel mountain chain of Provence. The inalterably beautiful day glides toward death like a woman who gradually weakens and fades without withering. The golden flow which little by little trickles in the sky seems to be distilled from the twisted trunks of the umbrella pines. The hour is already too far advanced for their branches to project a shadow upon the ground resembling a knot of vipers, but their massive presence thickens the subdued light and prepares the arrival of evening. We walk with indistinct step on a carpet of resinous needles so that our gait has the elastic appearance of phantoms. On the horizon, the mingled sea and sky are as wan and damp as lovers lost in a swoon. No sound is heard: in this silence, the trees settle and rest. My father is just as I knew him in the last years of his life, during the slow, insidious invasion of disease and death; wearing a flowing suit of clothes in light flannel, his long figure is etched in gray profile against the tree trunks and in black against the sky. He holds in his hand a thin flexible cane that looks rather like an equilibrist's balance, and his childlike eyes of faded blue consider the world through the wrinkled mask of an old man with drooping mustaches. I know that he is very close to me; I could describe his apparel down to the smallest detail; I know that he is melancholy, a little sullen, filled at this moment with the grief of a sorcerer who believes himself to have failed at the experiment of his lifetime, but I do not see him for we are walking side by side without ever turning our heads toward each other, and our eyes are fixed on the same point of the horizon. He speaks hesitantly and the words that he pronounces share the quality of almost all that resound in dream; they do not arrive from outside to strike our ears but vibrate within ourselves, for sleepers hear with their arteries, their entrails, and not with the organs of hearing that serve in waking and disclose foreign sounds; and just as there is a "white voice," a discoloration of the voice by affliction and anguish, it seems that there also exists a "white ear," a discoloration of hearing by dream, in which you receive nothing more than specters of sound.

Suddenly, I see my father extend toward the horizon his large hand strewn with pale brown spots and missing a finger that he had cut off long ago as an act of defiance, because a woman he loved claimed that he was incapable of inflicting the slightest suffering on himself for her

sake. And since the ring finger was later crushed in a door shut by wind
in the course of a violent storm, this hand of an executed criminal
assumes in my dream the aspect of an anatomical preparation, tanned
by acids, preserved in alcohol, and only missing the nail scars to be the
relic of a crucified hand. The sky in its entirety has turned red, the warm
red that flushes the cheeks of a child excited by play and running, and
this lively color finally helps me to accurately remember the words that
my father vaguely pronounced just now: it was a question of the infinite
variety of the shades of red placed between violet and magenta, and
especially this latter nuance which recurs continually in even his slightest
remark with the whispered sound of velvet. Gradually, the warm
coloration of the sky becomes at once more gorgeous and more somber:
we are in the midst of an oxblood cathedral propped up by the black and
irregular vaults of the pine branches. At the end of an alley formed by
two rows of parallel trunks, which are no longer those of the trees
familiar in the south of Europe, recalling instead in their soaring height
and colossal structure the cedars of Asia, we behold, in the distance, a
line of twenty-five individuals arrayed in brown or dirty gray, whose
long overcoats seem to be cut from sackcloth or drugget. From afar,
their faces form only a succession of pale stains; you can guess neither
their sex nor their age, but I know without counting that they are
twenty-five, neither one more nor less, and that this has nothing to do
with a mere figure but with a number, a fatal necessity that has been
imposed upon them and without which the universal order would be
overthrown. These poor wretches (for I know that they weep) simultaneously step forth between the trunks of the great cedars and fall into a
single kneeling line, in such a way that from our vantage point we can
only see twenty-five left profiles variously bowed. And one by one,
beneath the shock of who knows what invisible ax, those twenty-five
heads roll on the ground, disappear between the gigantic trunks of the
lofty trees opposite them, and rapidly descend the invisible slope that

goes down to the sea. But the twenty-five torsos remain upright, strongly borne up by their knees set in earth, while the rising tide of blood covers over the horizon, the world, and ourselves in one immense incarnadine surge that nothing can ever again withstand.

The Blue Child

I'm following a sunken path, bordered with thorny and deeply rooted hedges. Willows and lopped young elms create a pale green bower above my head; and the tender leaves are so thick and opulent that fragments of sky only appear in very gentle blue snatches, like the flowers of the forget-me-not amidst their foliage. The ground is muddy, full of deep ruts; beneath the grass, alongside the hedge, you can hear the murmuring of a rivulet, its coolness exhaled like a fragrance. At the foot of a large slightly yellowish willow, with roots lengthening over the moss like a large gaunt hand, I discover something which seems to be the hood of a blue mushroom, and which is none other than the sky-colored cap of an infant buried to his chin in damp earth. He is doll-sized and as flexible as a newborn. His round face, of a limpid paleness, recalls the bluish tint of milk skimmed of its cream; his eyes are of lake-water blue and so large that they seem ready to burst, like air-bubbles expanded in the extreme; he is squeezed into strange blue swaddling clothes adorned with short fringe; only his tiny mouth is pink, of the lovely pink of a Bengal rose strayed amidst so much sky. I pull him away from the ground like a beetroot, without hurting him, along with his roots of an almost black blue ending in slender fibrilla of the palest sky blue. He is very clean: the muddy ground hasn't left the slightest trace on his clothing or on the tops of his weak, clenched fists. For fear that he might catch cold, I swiftly gather a handful of dried grass, use it to cushion the hollow of my left arm, and set him down, as if in a nest, this infant who sleeps quietly with eyes wide opened, his head supported against my heart. But he grows animated, his lips part, and I am suddenly awakened by his sweet cry, his sharp cry, like the delightful cry of the swallow.

Wax Candles in the Cathedral

I stand at the foot of an enormous boulder, which rises sheer upwards and serves as a pedestal for a cathedral. The lofty rock is reddish brown in color, baked over and over again by the suns of millennial summers; clinging plants weave through its crevices with gentle and sinuous persistence as the wind sways abundant tufts of flowers against its tawny sides. The church for which it serves as a base is a seventeenth-century cathedral, chiseled in white marble by a baroque architect, a follower of Bernini: there is something theatrical about its structure; certain aspects of its bell turrets, so like the delicate and firm buds of white roses, recall, as often do small churches in Lower Austria, memories of marzipan sculptures slowly relished at village fairs, and dancing figures of bishops and martyrs twine a hedge around the facade or whirl about its two towers. No monumental staircase, no ramp connects the lone cathedral to the ground; only, deep within a tunnel, a narrow pass hollowed in the base of the summit, inconspicuous as the trace of a worm in a fruit, are some steep, uneven steps blasted from the rock, which climb straight up and lead into the nave by means of a sort of trap door, sculpted like a tomb. The stairwell is so narrow that both of my shoulders brush the walls; this contact with the stone is deadly chill. When I finally emerge into the heart of the nave, it is completely empty and very dark, but this gloom is not pure, created only by an absence of light; it seems softened, assuaged by a myriad of wavering gauze curtains, formed by masses of hanging steam, motionless, but without warmth or fragrance. Only the right transept is profusely lit by millions of candles and I dart there with the fluttering, hesitant approach of moths.

The candles rise tier upon tier alongside the wall, arranged hierarchically like the hosts of angels. There are candles as frail and flexible as women's fingers; others, wider, yet still very thin, like those you buy for small change in churches to illuminate God's pathway; still others have the shape of candles held during first communion or the taking of the veil; and there are some more massive, more weighty, a pallid arsenal of contrition and mourning, not unlike those paraded by the black penitents in Italy when they bury their dead. Finally, some have the almost monstrous girth of votive candles offered by sailors who have escaped from shipwreck, reminiscent of the diameter of masts; and some, at the furthest end, have the look of venerable trees with smooth trunks stripped of all their bark to permit the revelation of their soft white flesh. They are so wide that you can barely encircle them with your arms and so lofty that their trunks are lost in the penumbra, where their flame burns from very far away like a hanging lamp. These tapers do not dispel the darkness, but gleam in it like stars in the depth of night. They do not warm the chill and slightly acrid atmosphere of the church. A tall young woman stands motionless in a sort of apse, in the midst of this hall ablaze with candles. She is very beautiful and radiates a serene majesty. Her feet, her hands are nude, her light brown face is nude beneath her dark chestnut hair. Her wide, billowing skirt has the blue black shade of an ocean stirred by the wind; the heavy fabric cascades from her flanks to her knees, from her knees to her feet in deep, frozen waves which flow black upon black, shadows upon shadows, and blend with the density of the darkness. Her hands emerging from her somber sleeves seem to hover in the air, appeared from nowhere, suddenly arrived only to bless. I do not know if this is a living woman or only a statue: a scar beginning at her left temple descends to the corner of her grave lips, but perhaps this is a simple chink, like those cleaving the empty skulls of porcelain dolls. She does not breathe, but her veiled breast and her nude palms have the ineffable sweetness that belongs only to the flesh. She is propped against what seems to me a drapery traversed with great vertical folds, but upon a closer look, I see that this is actually a dress with deep pleats, like the fluting of columns, and that the tall standing woman is propped against the legs of a tall seated woman whose immense knees overreach the church vault and vanish in all directions into the night.

I hold myself upright before this goddess; I invoke her with arms upraised in a gesture of prayer, as are hers in a gesture of benediction. Something very deep within me advises me to name her mother, or rather *mothers,* as if that perfect face were reflected for all time in an endless play of mirrors, or rather, as if she were the last link in an infinite chain of goddesses, arranged one behind the other, increasingly indistinct and dreadful. But I also know that she is sweet as the honey from the latest gathering. I know that she differs from me only in majesty and power, that a blood similar to my own rests in her great cold veins, that she is neither foreign nor superior to all, but that she is, at once and most strangely, at the trembling surface of things, as well as in the most secret fiber of their heart.

I feel compelled to add a candle to that display of flames; besides, I understand that to fail in this obligation would be worse than sacrilege: this crime would bring disaster. But I look in vain all around me in search of a sacristan or a woman hiring out chairs; the church is empty and no one is there to sell me a candle. I begin to follow once again the flight of stairs hollowed from the rock; I race down the steep, slippery steps, holding on, in order not to fall, to the even more slippery walls. I remember that outside, in the square at the foot of the summit, I had glimpsed not long ago a little lodge built of slender laths painted green, where they sold candles, *ex-votos* made of wax, and gingerbread hearts. I hurry, anxious that six o'clock might toll from the church belfry, for I know that the shops close at six in the evening.

Outside, it is still broad daylight even though the sun is absent from the sky. The street is a deep, cool well, surmounted by a clear square of blue daylight. The lodge, pressed against the boulder, still offers its display of cakes and objects made of wax. A fat woman, who used to sell butter and chickens in a shop in my neighborhood, is seated near an orange-water fountain in the middle. She is huge and stricken with breast cancer; her left bosom has been recently amputated, leaving her serge bodice irregularly molded. She is as jovial as ever and thanks me cheerfully when I purchase from her a handful of candles, long slender candles adorned with a spiral of gilded paper. But when I make for the low concealed doorway to the staircase hewn from stone, I no longer recognize any sign of the dark opening. The narrow pass has closed together; the massive summit is nothing more than a single smooth block. No pathway will ever again lead into the heart of the cathedral, henceforth inaccessible, and the marble edifice seems to detach lightly from its rocky pedestal and, like a great white bird, hovers in the air.

The Animal's Rich Repast

I am in Paris, at the Museum of the Orangerie, where an exhibition of all the animals on earth has been organized. But this is not an exhibition open to the public, for only a few rare visitors are privileged to gaze upon these beautiful, haughty animals, and no chain, no ring, no iron railing separates man from God's other savage creatures. This is a *congress* of the lords of the jungle and desert but also a banquet in the Roman style, where the patricians with powerful jaws, lying on their sides, carelessly sprawled on carpets struck by their long striped tails, advance their claws toward large silver dishes set on the floor. They thrust their muzzles into cups brimming with blood red wine, and the enormous barbarous meats are prepared with the same gorgeous display as a Renaissance banquet.

The first hall is dedicated to the tigers, to panthers, to lions as russet as sand, to bears as white as glaciers. The second hall is devoted to the birds: macaws, parakeets, eagles, falcons, tits, blackbirds, goldfinches, sea gulls, canaries from the islands, skylarks, storks, and crows, all the feathers of the hedgerow and ploughed fields, all the wings of the rain forest, the marsh, and the rocks. Set on perches, they voraciously await the solemn meal which should be served to them, and it is I who am entrusted with offering them the silver gilt platters laden with grain, fish, flies, or earthworms, or the lumps of meat torn by birds of prey. I pass between the rows of golden perches, holding a silver platter balanced in the palm of each hand, and the large-bellied vultures that dung like harpies, the eagles with widespread pinions, haggard and magnificent as if they had emerged from an imperial fresco, the long carrier pigeons in traveling garb, and hummingbirds the size of precious stones hasten and plunge their heads into the platters seasoned with glowworms. Suddenly, this Olympus of birds, this Pantheon of wild animals, is emptied, swept away as if by enchantment, and I find myself on the terrace of the Orangerie on an autumn day, near a lounge chair where an ailing old man lies under a plaid blanket. His majestic hands of a former blacksmith are placed on his bony knees and, with a slow, distracted, sorrowful gesture, he caresses a cat with patchy yellow fur, a scrawny, mangy cat, trembling with fever and certain to die soon.

The Wild Horses

A heath with a scattering of tall trees. Something undefinable in the atmosphere convinces me that we are not in France but somewhere in England, perhaps Richmond Park or the gently rolling countryside near Windsor. However, nothing here recalls the luxuriant opulence of English greenery: the color of the grass is not fresh but faded to the gray brown you find at the end of torrid afternoons that prematurely bestow upon the earth the dusty look of autumn. All sensation of stifling heat is, however, excluded from this beige dream, just as feelings of cold were from the earlier white dream, and perhaps it is worth mentioning here that one rarely experiences physical cold or heat in dreams, seldom yawns, hardly ever feels hunger, and almost never is subject to the throes of desire with the full force of its violence. In dream, one crosses the desert, lies down in the snow, occasionally eats or makes love, but with something of the floating detachment of the gods or ghosts. If sensations gain the upper hand over visions, if one chokes or faints away, it is because the dream is drawing near to the frontiers of awakening, where the outstretched hand of suffering or exhausting joy already waits. But I have no reason to believe that someone profoundly asleep has ever experienced indigestion in the midst of a dream.

The most complex dreams are brief, or rather, neither long nor short, but unfold outside of time. On the other hand, any faithful description of a dream must necessarily be slow and meticulous since this is a matter of amassing the words that will allow the reader to try the weight of the imponderable, to slip in through a maze of often remote analogies to the heart of an unknown world and become adapted each time to the special climate and the strange, new scent of the dream. This heath that might have been nothing more than some corner of a public garden in England, dedicated to the evolutions of soldiers on parade or to the amorous slumber of Sunday couples, has, by means of a nuance of sinister gray, conjured the desolate plain where the old King Lear roamed before the thunderstorm burst and the gleam of lightning flashes appeared to suddenly illuminate for him the landscape of his undoing. This allusion, which might seem at first glance to be nothing but a literary embellishment, is the only one that can help me evoke the impression of isolation and fleeting majesty produced by these endlessly outstretched spaces carpeted with heather, which provides the sole touch of autumnal color. Perhaps such ideas are summoned by the presence of a character who will soon make his entrance and is never far away whenever I dream deeply about my life. For some time now, I have been in the middle of this heath, the solemnity of which is actually unrelated to any particularly sorrowful or sinister detail, and where even stand, here and there, two or three of those little peddler's kiosks, cheerfully constructed of light wood, where hawkers of toys and lemonade supply children with opaline marbles, jump ropes, and sponge cakes that always grate beneath the teeth because they have been exposed to the free wind and sprinkled with dust. But on that day, everything was still, motionless under an illumination of clouds and dusk, and no breath stirred over this deserted heath.

It was, however, the presence of whirlwinds of white dust that revealed to me the outline of a broad road, crossing straight through the landscape, converging north and south with the vague bounds of the empty horizon. It was not the wind that raised the dust, but horses, a horde, an army of horses all galloping in the same direction, all rushing from my left down the desolate road that crosses the heath. They seem to have emerged from the confines of one horizon only to dash into another, and the anxious, impetuous attack through the long plain has for them only the duration of a lightning flash. Horses without riders, horses mounted by vague, anonymous figures, camouflaged with dust, sweat, and weariness, like athletes who all end up wearing the same exhausted-looking face and the same gray clothing as a race draws to the finish. Riders in khaki, in beige, in iron gray, wearing those turbid hues that only belong to the muddy torrent of a river, or to advancing armies, and which do nothing to reveal the identity or origins of what must surely be men. Nothing, moreover, especially indicates that these are soldiers, or if they are charging toward a target or fleeing from an enemy. And most of these horses, with saddles but rid of their human tyrants, were galloping madly, freely, spurred on by some unknown danger. Still others, without saddle, without bridle, were nude as the horses snorting on the plains of Eden during the first days of creation. Brown horses, russet horses, horses of a dirty white, dappled horses, gray horses, horses galloping in unison, massive as the displacement of waves, yellowish horses billowing on the white road without the sound of hooves, without neighing, without the clacking of bits, in the dreadful absence of sound that accompanied cowboy raids dashing across the screen at the time of silent films. Gradually, this silence becomes modulated within me like a solemn music; the throbbing of my blood scans a sort of violent and raucous funeral march and I dimly understand that this savage drove of wild animals is hastening inevitably toward a chasm, that the horizon is a slope, and that slope the edge of an abyss where they will roll to the bottom.

In the midst of this multitude of rebellious horses, all galloping without master even when they still drag a rider stuck to the saddle, a large white horse mounted by a man, also wearing the uniform of gray dust and whose face is no more visible to my eyes than if he were wearing a mask, clearly stands out in relief against the shifting background of croups and manes. The animal mounted by the man resists the thrust of this horizontal surge, contained as a rising tide; she flees above, with a leap that reaches the sky. She falls again and rolls on the ground without loosening the rider fixed to her sides; by means of her own bulk, she escapes from the countless tread of the horde, which instinctively divides around her as if she were a rock. Once again, she rebounds like an elastic animal and climbs so far into the sky that she cannot avoid breaking to pieces when she falls again. But she does not break, and the game or the contest continues, for I do not know whether the rider is struggling to escape from her or forces her into this strange aerial dance, whether I am present at a battle or at the practice session of an archangel's riding school. Meanwhile, the other horses have burst through the imaginary barriers that held them in the bed of the road; they rear; they bound; they scatter in disorder across the heath, overturning the lemonade vendors' pavilions with their chests, and their feet raise the dust and blades of dry grass. Only then do feelings of regal and sacral horror cede within me to fear and a longing to run away. Suddenly, a large bony hand alights on my shoulder; I sense next to me a man of imposing stature and, in that elderly man, I recognize my dead father. And he tells me in his cheerful voice in which I guess the radiance of a good-natured smile:

> "It is dangerous here, don't you think?"

> As if he would have told me:

> "It is lovely out today."

The Wind through the Grass

As this dream begins, the wind does not blow through the grass but through the stones. We are in the middle of a strange, rocky construction, shaped like a hive that might have gigantic termites for its bees; the vaulted walkways and the dome hollowed in soft stone seem to be made of a series of combs of tufa rather than of honey. The smell that steals around us is distasteful and rancid like that of black cakes crumbling to dust within tombs. The room in which we find ourselves is as gloomy as a funeral hut and the conical vault resembles the interior of a mitre; but it is not completely dark inside, even though windows are nowhere in evidence and not a single lamp is in sight. A series of round corridors encircles the central apse, which thus resembles the hub of a wheel or the hollow core of a stone tree. Slightly oblique walkways, symmetrically sprung from our present site, cut these labyrinthine galleries through and through, augmenting the prevailing impression of tedious sameness and vertigo, and everything around us stirs imperceptibly, as if nothing, at our present depth, could withstand the earth's motion.

I am shut in here with the young man and woman with whom I lived in Venice in a previous dream; the young man has put on a raincoat of black oilcloth over his discolored plaid suit, fading into indistinct patterns, and the young woman is wrapped in a peignoir of frothy white tulle. Thick snowflakes still adhere to her lace frills and, even though it is very cold in the deep cavern where we find ourselves, the snow melts little by little and trickles away in gray pools, so that the slender young woman has the look of a fountain statue set in a damp grotto. With meticulous curiosity, the young man scrutinizes each of the numerous little hexagonal cavities in the wall, which presents from top to bottom a succession of columbaria niches, and he needs finger only a bit of the ash which each of these black mouths contains in order to know whether the debris of a man, a rat, or a destroyed bird is in question. But the young woman rises despairingly on her Louis XV heels, because she is searching for the remains of her stillborn child that someone had left somewhere beneath the vaults. She does not find him, for she is blind. Tired to death, she soon sinks down on a granite block in the middle of the burial chamber and, with infinite patience, upon her knees pressed together, she places her opened and joined palms that still seem to bear the weight of something vanished. She is not totally abandoned, for an ancient tortoise leaves the wall and humbly licks her foot like a good, faithful dog, and the wretched woman's warm tears drop down on the unfeeling carapace. I seize the young woman's inert hands in an attempt to restore them to life, but they are ice-cold, as if all of her life's warmth had passed into her tears. Between two sobs, she confides in me that her child had been alive, but someone had strangled the poor innocent because he never managed to learn how to smile.

The gusts of wind chase each other like clamorous ghosts through the corridors, scattering the ashes from the tombs; suddenly, the enormous muffled thunder of an avalanche rumbles overhead, and we realize that a monstrous mass of snow has just collapsed above us, sweeping away in its descent the earth and loose rock from the hill beneath which we are prisoners, irrevocably filling up the outlets that we were hoping to leave by. It is clear to us that we had entered this morning in the capacity of simple tourists, and if we are now alone, it is because the guardian had left us a few moments ago, the sooner to restore the electricity that had just gone out, but we realize that the guardian will never again be able to return to search for us, and we feel the first stirrings of alarm. An easy ramp, discovered at the back of the hall, allows us to climb to the floor above in quest of an emergency door: we find only a room exactly like the one we just left but pierced with countless windows furnished with panes so opaque and thick that you have difficulty discerning whether or not these windowpanes are stones. You cannot open them and the young man and his girlfriend bloody their fists in a vain attempt to smash them. Leaving my companions behind, I go down again to the lower floor of the cavern, but there I am confronted with nothing but a black and suffocating confusion of half-collapsed galleries, where I am forced to slide flat on my belly, beating my way through the stones and fine mold with blows of my head, and this protracted crawling on the cold ground destroys my clothing to the point that I am soon totally nude.

Unexpectedly, with no premonition of deliverance, I am conscious of being bathed in daylight. Emerged from the cavern, still shivering with the cold endured in the sepulchral chamber, I shake off the dust that adheres to my wanly nude body, clings to my hair, and sets upon my brow a sign like that of Ash Wednesday. But here in open space, in the open air, the whistling of the wind is so strong that my ears take fright and I make a move to return to my tomb. But I grow accustomed to this din of storm, of speed, and of laughter, and I walk forward, as falteringly as a woman cured by miracle, beneath this violent sky that snaps like sailcloth. I turn my back on the hill where the subterranean cavities are concealed under a green embankment; I am halfway down a landscape of valleys with a river at its bottom. The banks, the hillocks, the hollows, the opposing planes of the land are but a single, undulant facing of new grass, where no flower is mingled. It is a March morning, a paschal morning, and the gray water of the thaw has gone to nurture the greenness of the grass. Somewhere, an invisible sun warms again the still sharp atmosphere of a day that has barely climbed out of earth and the harsh purity of the landscape recalls the uncompromising nobility of a sixteen-year-old's mind. The wind's friendly force travels through the meadow like an express; here and there, cows and sheep raise their heads and ruminate this heavy, familiar uproar. I have stretched out right in the middle of the grass in order to better feel the trembling caress of the young blades against my nape, against my cheek, against my leg, and I throw back my head to better drink the white sky. Suddenly, a stronger gust of wind bears away, like a large balloon, the hill of just a moment ago, which now resembles an immense and delicate Easter egg of pale green, with, at the very top, the young man and young woman, who have finally managed to open the windows and cheerfully wave their white handkerchiefs in a sign of farewell.

The Reflecting Pool in the Church

Death, standing in a garden, plays the violoncello. This garden flowers and grows green inside a cloister, within four walls of evenly trimmed boxwood. The vaults, the green black pilasters, the cloister's springing arches are all sculpted from this vigorous, living substance and the branches, continually mutilated to comply with the exactions of monastic architecture, exude a scent acrid as fever and love. Standing in the garden, death plays the violoncello. A green carpet of pale grass covers the ground, irregularly molded with hillocks which are perhaps tombs, so that the strings of the great instrument seem to communicate immediately with the heart of the dead, and it is sorrowful to reflect that this community might not hear such solemn music, which some of them must surely have dreamed of their whole life through. Death is a skeleton stripped of flesh, but a very thin and transparent skin clings to her sharp bones, exactly in the manner of cellophane used to protect dried fruit arrived from across the seas, and a little rouge, where the cheeks would be, has been rubbed over the yellow parchment. Despite her far-famed voracity, her svelte silhouette recalls that of a society woman who never eats her fill for fear of growing fat. A velvet cloak fastened to her left collarbone partially drapes her in its ample blue folds. She plays with the obstinacy of a mute, with unwavering attention, and her bare skull is adorned with a garland of faded boxwood.

Five young women are seated at the feet of Death, their legs casually stretched before them in the grass, as if for a picnic gathering, or folded under their wide billowing skirts which recall the spreading corollas of flowers. The first wears lemon yellow, and the second a dress of flaxen blue, the third a pink dress, and the fourth a dress of lavender, but the fifth woman's dress is the color of daybreak. All sit calmly, as if they dared not move for fear of creasing their Sunday best; their slender arms are lightly passed around the waist or shoulder of their companions, and they whisper insignificant secrets to each other in low voices. Their backs are turned to the terrible performer, nonetheless, they are not unaware of her presence and her nearness renders them only slightly more pale. From time to time, Death leans her bow against the delicate neck of one of the beauties; then the young woman throws back her head while letting escape from her throat a lament as sweetly piercing as the highest note of some unknown scale. Seeing me pass by, the young women call out to me, beckon, but I'm wearing my everyday clothes and I'm pressed for time, for the afternoon approaches its end and I'm in a hurry to enter the church.

My only care is traversing the cloister and I enter an inner courtyard which contains nothing but an abandoned well with its edge of old marble, zigzagged with cracks. I would like to draw water to drink, but only a fragment of a broken cup hangs from the towrope, and I enter the church with all of my thirst.

It is very dark inside so that the shadow seems to spread an artificial chill. The wide-open door-leaves, sculpted with mermaids and nude women, allow a little of the music and the twilight to enter the apse; you can see just enough to grope about and, since this large empty space contains neither benches nor chairs nor alms boxes, the most one risks is knocking into a column. The almost round church closely imitates the interior plan of Saint Peter's in Rome; it is scarcely less vast and side chapels distend the contours of the choir like hernias. The invisible altar occupies its center, raised higher by a shallow step, no doubt accessible to the hesitant tread of the ancient prelates come to officiate there. A more narrow staircase allows me to reach a high gallery, which should be in white marble if only it were bright enough to tell. I kneel before the balustrade of polished Carrara marble and prop my hands on the smooth ledge.

I am alone in the church, but something is lying down before the altar, beneath a veil of black velvet. I know that this something is my self, or rather, my reflection. The black and white flagstones of the pavement, which transform the floor of the church into a chessboard where the black squares no doubt mark the tombs of the damned and the white squares those of the blessed dead, by chance reflected my passing image and someone threw this flap of dark velvet over it to hinder its escape, just as the mirrors are covered in the homes of the dead. My imprisoned reflection stirs and throbs beneath the black veil and the long shape prostrated before the altar is reminiscent of a nun in devotion or a cadaver being absolved of the sin of having lived. But the veil does not stop trembling and moving like wings and conjures thoughts of some large velvety bat, collapsed there after having unintentionally put out all of the lights with one slightly brushing contact, apprehensive and tentative. Little by little this veil contracts, becomes thinner, finally taking on the soft bronze shade of a dead leaf. Soon, only a great marrowy pool remains on the pavement of the church, pallidly golden like the essential oil that seeps from the heart of palm trees, and from which there would be sufficient to draw in order to rekindle all of the lamps. But no one will ever again rekindle the lamps, for all the sacristans are dead, and the great useless pool trembles and shimmers in the penumbra grown increasingly black, while the sound of the organ reverberates in the vacant church, replacing the strains of the violoncello.

The House of the Pale Women

I've bought a ticket at the counter of the Sauvebelin funicular at Lausanne. I am seated in a rather dark compartment with a young woman whose name and face I forget. The funicular is climbing an almost imperceptible slope that is none other than the roofing of a cathedral. This roofing of gray tiles is rendered singularly slippery by the presence of pine needles fallen from tall trees that grow between the sheets of slate as if in the crevices of rocks, in the manner of those flower beds of highly pleasing weeds sown by the wind on the rooftops of village churches. Italianate gardens, rising terrace upon terrace, come after the forest: through the forest of old trees and the quincunx, one descries the great white dome that crowns the choir of this gigantic cathedral and stands out in profile against the horizon like an entirely round mountain of smooth stone. The funicular lets us both out at the foot of that great eminence, like a hive or a Mohammedan tomb, then the unknown traveler vanishes and I go my way unaccompanied.

After a few steps, I find myself in front of a chalet pressed to the bosom of the mountain. It is built of gleaming pine board that still retains a resinous scent and color. An exterior staircase leads to a long latticed gallery: I push a half-opened door and easily enter a narrow dark corridor that commands several rooms. But these rooms are empty, devoid of furniture; this deserted house is, in its entirety, haunted by a sense of a disquieting, inexplicable presence, and I have to gather all of my courage to climb the few concealed stairs that lead to the first floor.

Up there, the landing forms a sort of square antechamber with walls of polished pine. No furniture, apart from a few benches of bare wood. You breathe in a faint but insistent odor of varnish. The floor is made of coarse beams covered over with sawdust, and the general effect of this room irresistibly recalls waiting rooms, the provincial police stations in Russian villages or the customs buildings on the frontiers of the small Balkan states. This stifling yet chill place emits an almost unbearable feeling of resigned boredom, stupefaction, of mute disquietude disguised as helpless amazement.

Two women are seated face to face on the benches of hard wood. Both are still young, very pale, very thin, a bit bony, with strong, pensive hands, and broad shoulders outlined beneath their dresses of uncertain color—brown, dried plum, wine dregs—that turn an unclean black in this room deprived of light. They lean their somnolent heads against the walls of varnished wood, and their flaxen hair is so luminous that it appears white. Both have beautiful eyes rimmed with rose circles, which create the effect of being worn with tears, but their thin lips lack all gentleness; their heavy chins advance with an expression of stubborn disgust, and bitter folds deepen at the base of their nose, the corners of their mouth; and one wonders in vain whether these two women, set at the intersection of malice and misfortune, are victims or criminals, whether they are to be pitied or feared. They resemble each other to the point that you might take one of the two twins for the simple reflection of her companion, as if one of the walls were occupied by a large mirror. But this is wrong, for while the woman on the left rests her hands and palms heavily on her knees in an attitude of weighted weariness and infinite dullness, the woman on the right automatically cradles and rocks an infant as wan and emaciated as herself. Perhaps she is a trifle paler, a trifle more beautiful than her sister, and her eyes are a little brighter. Her child is livid, with traces of green and yellow at the commissures of lips and eyelids, and stirs no more than a dead child, but one hears him crying feebly, and his low, monotonous lament recalls the cicada's hoarse moan. This woman, who has reached the extreme of paleness, tells me I have no idea what, something that I do not understand, that I do not even hear, as if I were deaf or as if she were contented with simply moving her lips in the manner of the mute. Not for a moment does she stop rocking her child between her strong hands with the same indifferent motion, without tenderness, without sweetness, and only her bust moves slightly between her motionless head and knees. Her companion has also not changed her attitude: she remains seated, her hands on her knees, her torso rigid, her head thrown back a bit, with the compact, impenetrable fixity of stone.

The proximity of these two women frightens me, and, at all costs, I wish to flee this antechamber that opens only upon a black corridor. The moment that I gropingly risk my way through this passage without light, I notice that the walls to the left and right are pierced with doorways, but these doors are irremediably locked, and my hands are worn out from vainly searching for latches in the darkness. At last, a knob agrees to turn in my hand; I enter a room in all respects exactly like the schoolrooms set up on the highest floors of the country houses where our childhood slipped away, with its bare walls, geography maps, its shelves of books with damaged pasteboard bindings, and the desk splattered with ink blots to which one added legs to make them all the more resemble noxious spiders. A young boy in a sailor's suit is seated at this table; he can't be more than fourteen years of age, and yet I recognize, beneath this disguise of an adolescent who has shot up too fast, the man whom I had so much, so dearly loved. I experience a tender joy at finding him again here, in this unfamiliar guise, at this age, when not having met me yet, he has not yet begun to make me suffer, but this joy is immediately mixed with anxiety because of the defiant and resolute expression in his eyes. He is slender and delicate, pale, but with a fresh pallor that has nothing in common with the lividity of the two women who wait on the bench on the landing; his eyelids are ringed with dark circles, his features are tense like those of an overworked schoolboy before an exam, and the draft created by my entrance scatters sheets of lined paper throughout the room. He gets up: he comes towards me mysteriously, a finger to his lip, like the young god of silence in Grecian low reliefs. He murmurs: "We have to leave right away. To get away from here. These people are wicked; they live only on game."

And he takes me by the hand. We leave the room, go down a hidden staircase to avoid passing the two malicious or unfortunate women. We soon find ourselves once again in the dark corridor of the beginning, then the latticed gallery that enframes, beyond the garden, a somewhat contrived Alpine landscape like those forged only in Bavaria. We cross through narrow garden beds and parterres; it is the beginning of spring or the end of autumn; no flower, no thread of grass emerges from the rich, carefully raked soil where our feet sink deeply. It is mild and gentle out: large red corollas just like stars tremble on branches still or already stripped of their leaves; a chill and intermittent blast blows through the powerful vertebrae of those trees deprived of sap. We walk side by side, with hands tightly clasped, reassured by the fresh contact of our bare fingers, but in a hurry to descend terrace after terrace and to finally leave this garden planted on the rooftop of a cathedral. No one pursues us; the terrifying blast turns gentle when it caresses our hair; but the emptiness, the very silence conveys some incomprehensible threat, worse than any presence, and who knows whether our enemies are invisible? Suddenly, the explosion of an alarm bell resounds behind us, and we turn around in time to see the reeling sides of the gigantic dome that overhangs the chalet, as if the bells ringing in the lantern tower of the dome were enough to shake that enormous white sphere. At that very moment, a mob comes from all sides, invades the terraces, and one hears the dull thudding of thousands of bare feet resound on the soft earth. These emaciated people, clothed in tatters, armed with bayonets, make you think of rioters rather than bandits, and certain details of their costume and wild headdress recall the populace during the great, momentous days of the Revolution. They rush into the garden like an irresistible avalanche that climbs rather than descends, overturning barriers, breaking the bare branches that snap violently beneath the onslaught of the human storm, expunging the towlines at the edge of the thicket, finally hurling down the chalet, which yields to their pressure and which they trample underfoot like the wooden paling of a fairground stall, amidst a storm cloud of screams. But the young boy and I are already on the main road, in open country, safe and delivered, and we hurry our steps to push yet further away from misfortune.

The Pathway at Twilight

The adolescent and I are once more on the road together. We are no longer holding hands, but we are still walking side by side. We are in the Alps, on one of those paths through the mid-mountains set equidistant between the valley and the glaciers. To our right, the green slope plunges out of view, strewn with massive rocks that resemble the black croups of motionless cattle. From time to time, a narrow handrail extends along the path, separating us from the void, and then our road looks like a balcony winding around the mountainside, a terrace from which one could observe the sky. This sky is green, of the drained green which is the most livid nuance that a blue sky can adopt; thin sharp stars, like needle points, pierce the sky from depths that one guesses to be infinite; they glimmer without advancing along the trail of evening, and the even layer of brightness remains stagnant, changing in neither density nor thickness. We are making our way between day and night, in the brief interval between the two flood tides that by turns cover over space, each time sweeping away, like the drowned, several hundred of the dead. This state of melancholy and majestic equilibrium will last until the end of our walk and until the middle of the dream. We move forward, but no shadow is cast before us or follows us along the road, and the twilight enfolds us like a transparent mist. We do not speak and it seems that even our hearts grow silent; our lungs have stopped inhaling and exhaling the evening air, and if I were to take my companion's wrist, I would no longer feel the reassuring din of his life against the pad of my finger. Only the sound of our steps still resounds in the silence, reverberating with the echo from the rocky wall, multiplied as if we were being followed by an invisible crowd. To our left, the rocky spur raises its vertical partition, harsh as a prison wall behind which fountains weep; and immense notches, hollowed by the rain, sketch indecipherable inscriptions on the smooth, bare stone. Rare pine trees appear here and there; the blades of grass glimpsed on the side of the precipice are not green, nor black, but uniformly discolored like those parcels of yellowed, desiccated moss that one finds in the back of flower shops. A cloud of very fine dust constantly rises from our feet to our knees, and the monotony of this mute walk conjures thoughts of the suffering in purgatory. A sudden bend in the road allows us to discover, still at a considerable distance, a modest village pressed down into the hollow of the mountain, with its cattle stalls resembling votive structures, its hovels covered with black tiles and plastered with pastry dough like funeral cakes, and the piercing church tower, overreaching the stony wall of the field of tombs. A large hay wagon passes us, driven by a stout man with a blue face. We hasten our steps, for the wind is rising; we are cold, and the blast goes through us as if we weren't even there. Suddenly, I stumble against a stone, and I fall as if I were beginning to kneel.

It is not a stone, but the corpse of a stillborn infant lying on its stomach and wrapped in brown sackcloth. The shapeless little body is tightly bound in swaddling, the fists are clenched, and the face frozen in the grimace made by infants on the verge of sneezing or crying. He is as pale as the Christ child, who smiles in churches at the time of Epiphany, but it is easy to see that he is not made of wax, but of pitiful, dead flesh. I take him in my arms with the utmost tenderness, for he is as fragile as glass, and the cold imparted to me from this infant, who has never lived, is keener than the cold of the night. In fact, night has begun to fall around us like some sort of snow, in immense gray flakes. We enter the village where the doors and windows of the low houses remain open to capture the last of the twilight, for the people here are very poor and the lamps are only lit at the last possible moment; a dried fish hangs at a crossroads: it is the sign of Christ. We slip on the paving stones, slick with liquid manure: I am afraid of dropping this infant who, nonetheless, runs no risk of crying; and my tender concern for this corpse is perhaps more uneasy than it would be for the living. Occasionally, at the turning of a narrow lane, an ox passes his head through a stable vent and blows on our faces his mild breath resembling the scent of dung. I am going to leave the dead infant at the guardhouse that has the appearance of a telegraph office: there are strips of printed forms that are tugged and spread out like rolls of toilet paper in water closets. A man smoking his pipe has opened the door to the stove and is engrossed in toasting bread on the end of a long fork, and, in order to attract his attention, I tap a coin against the windowpane, while the black snow continues to drift down on me.

It is now completely dark: without my knowing how, they have taken the dead infant from my arms, and the young boy who has accompanied me is no longer there; he has evaporated with the final sigh of the light. I am boarding with the parish priest since there is no inn. I sleep in a garret, but I dine at the priest's table: this is more comfortable since the table is oval. The wooden staircase creaks when you set your foot there because of the rats which live in the planks, and I race downstairs just as I had in my childhood when I was afraid of the black landings where the carpet rod vaguely gleams, along with the copper knobs of blocked-up doors. I am right to be afraid, for the parish priest's servant has vowed to kill me. She is a woman of around forty years of age, very thin, with a livid face and a bitter grimace that tugs the corner of her mouth as if she were incessantly chewing on misfortune. Her long equine head is dressed with thin blond hair like bristles, wound into a meager chignon; her blue striped dress seems as faded as her pale eyes that seem etched in acid; she stares at me with fixed ill intent. Her hands are very cold and touch things with obscene, light contact; she hounds my steps unceasingly and I do not hear her walking since she has felt slippers. Just now, during dinner, she tried to strangle me, but I loosened her hands. She stands behind the back of my chair and I am forced to constantly keep an eye on her in the mirror. I have to murder her in order to prevent her from killing me. While she is clearing the table, I snatch a knife left on a plate; I throw it at her, aiming at her chest, in the way that knives are tossed in shooting galleries at traveling fairs. The dagger plunges deeply into her heart, and, if it were possible, she turns even paler; like a gargoyle, she opens her disgusting mouth, but she doesn't fall; she does not bleed; she does not scream or one doesn't hear her scream. She dissolves into the gray wallpaper, into the air thickened by the stove, into the twilight of the snow. And nothing is more terrifying than the sensation of having struck to death a miserable creature incapable of even bleeding.

The Flower Boxes

I am in a children's room fitted up at the top of an ancient country house. The room is heated by a stove with enamel tiles representing scenes from La Fontaine's *Fables,* and the likeness of a Louis XV shepherd playing the flute is fixed to the wall next to the large pipe, always a bit blackened, from which the smoke escapes. The room is round, for we are inside a tower. At least half the wall is taken up with six large windows with little crossbars of lead, which permit a view of the gray sky and the treetops in the garden. A doll, whose brains escape from a circular crack that twists around the cranium and descends to the base of the nose, is propped against an old gilded secretary, which holds a writing desk, a collection of postcards, and dust for drying letters. In a corner, an old prayer stool of soiled blue velvet has kneeled down before a Holy Virgin in ebony, standing on clouds with the horns of the moon breaking through, and a half-opened door communicates with a dark cabinet, where the ghosts enter and leave when the midnight hour strikes. Nothing has changed in this room in a house that I haven't revisited since the age of seven or eight and now long since destroyed by bombshells. The house is still as melancholy, as vast, as strange, and the rain which filters from cracks in the ceiling forms star-shaped pools on the carpet. Only, the entire width of the room is spanned by a cord, where they have hung eiderdowns to dry, freshly tinted in all the hues of the rainbow, namely vermilion, orange, violet, and yet other shades. These tones are of an admirable purity and candor, like those of some modern painting, and it seems that the spongy thickness of the partially fluffed quilts is transformed into a visual quality, saturated in color that the eye may finger and handle. A dozen large rubber balls, brilliantly colored, are arranged symmetrically on the carpet, green as grass. They look like those candies colored with aniline found in the glass jars of grocers and pharmacists in England, but like candies for giants or candies for gods, and the joy which the simple sight of these stout spheres—red, yellow, white or blue—procures for me is at once innocent and absolute, like that of the infant who laughs and watches the fringe on his cradle sway, or the invalid who stares, from morning to night, at the selfsame stain on his hospital wall becoming a rose.

A narrow stone step allows access to the deep windows, pierced very high into the thickness of the wall. Two long flower boxes adorn this sort of raised ledge, two cement boxes reinforced in the corners by iron hooks, like those seen on the balconies and terraces of cafes in the high season. But no flower emerges from them and these boxes seem to hold only carefully raked soil. Someone invisible explains to me that it is absolutely impossible to leave them where they are and directs me to place them aslant on the stone ledge, the head against the wall and the foot on the floor. Assisted by a worker whose face I do not see, I succeed in moving these heavy bulks fitted with light soil; to make room for them, I have to kick aside the dazzling spheres which shrivel, grow pale, and finally deflate like punctured balls. Once leaned like coffins loaded on a hearse, these heavy, oblong boxes reveal their contents and I notice that delicate green shoots are beginning to pierce the even surface of the soil in the box placed to my left: these thin-sown and slender blades of grass sketch a circle that vaguely evokes a woman's silhouette. I understand immediately that this box is prepared for me, that everything has been made ready for me to lie down as if in bed, discreetly, without having to empty the contents of soil, without disturbing the pattern traced on the surface, just as you carefully lie down between embroidered sheets. But I have no intention to stretch out there right away for I am not in the mood for sleeping. The box on the right is exactly like the box on the left, but it does not contain earth alone: the man whom I had so much loved is lying there. He is wearing somewhat rumpled gray clothes; at first, I am reassured by his wide-open eyes, but he is as still as a sleeper thrust far beyond his dreams, and this stillness is a clue that he is hardly alive. The narrow dimensions of the box compel him to press his arms to his side and the long thin hands crossed over his abdomen are reminiscent of the enormous claws of dejected birds that have spent their lives in captivity. The earth partially covers him, somewhat in the way that water sparingly poured into the bottom of a bathtub covers a nude man, and from time to time he pulls it up over himself like a sheet, with the determined and feeble gesture of invalids who are going to die. He breathes weakly but without effort: his slightly strained lips expose teeth that make me think, in spite of myself, of the jaws of the dead and of the fangs of vampires, who also shelter their blood-gorged sleep in coffins filled with earth, but he is so pale that you could open your veins without restoring to him the colors of life, and so icy cold that you could never warm him again by lying down on his heart. He speaks without moving his lips, in a very low voice, which I guess rather than hear. He tells me:

"You also have to give me some flowers. It's more comfortable."

I hadn't noticed that a large bouquet of flowers was placed on the desk in a bottle of blue glass. They are a little faded, perhaps because, until now, no one had paid the slightest attention to their timid, silent, and pallid appearance. These are simple delphiniums, but complicated and enlarged by intensive cultivation, of a very bright shade of azure that recalls the eyes of Siamese cats. I attempt to take some, but the withered petals only tenuously cling to their stems and shed in a sudden shower of blue dust upon the polished mahogany of the old secretary. I gather that dust and fill the hands of the sleeper with it. With a maniacal and instinctive gesture, he pulls it in toward the top of his chest, toward his throat, toward his face; he bathes in that dust spread over him and mingled with the damp earth that smells of death. His young worn face is deteriorated like those of marble statues too long exposed to inclement weather; and the large droplets of rain which fall one by one from the ceiling, flooding the room despite the white porcelain jugs laid out on the floor to receive them, roll heavily like tears over this gray impassive face.

The Woman Stricken with Leprosy

This is a pale nightmare. I dream that my left arm is overspread with leprosy, a leprosy as thick and scintillant as a crust of salt. My swollen arm does not hurt, but I find it as disgusting as a diseased animal next to which I am forced to lie down. And this monstrous arm, grown gigantic, crumbles like marble into dust, melts like snow, is decomposed into yielding dough, leaving me at last in the condition of those statues in the royal parks of France or Bavaria, drenched and mold-stained, amputated in riots yet continuing to bravely sketch some useless gesture, with their rotten hands next to them in the grass, forgotten like a pair of gloves. And I also resemble the frightful beggars in Levantine bazaars, who suddenly pull out from European jackets a bare shoulder with its dangling tip of dead flesh in order to prove beyond doubt that they are, indeed, the poorest of the poor, and that God has placed misfortune between work and their good will like a prohibition. My ruined arm flows away on the ground and forms a pool where the pus drips at regular intervals like the water of a clepsydra. I feel that this rottenness is sacred, at once a punishment and a sign. And like children who have cut their finger and suck the blood so nothing is lost, I pull out an aluminum spoon from the pocket of my traveling cloak, and I drink the water of this pool, as if I were receiving the sacrament of my own decay.

The Burnt House

The young boy and I are once again walking side by side, but my hand is not joined to his, and it is morning instead of being twilight. We are crossing through a landscape of long rippling plains, all waving with lakes and woodlands; and little valleys, planted with elms that lift mutilated branches, leave off unexpectedly to make room for a steep slope, glazed by the sun, that is replaced in turn by an endless stretch of national highway set flat against an embankment and lengthening through the countryside like a land surveyor's tape measure. We walk swiftly: the miles flow underfoot with almost miraculous speed, for we are little, not yet six or seven years of age. It is lovely out: the sun, shifting through the foliage, dapples our faces with dark shadows, while the breeze idly toys with the branches of large familiar trees whose names have not been taught to us yet. From time to time, we rest a moment to gather a leaf from the lowest branch, and, carefully, with tongues extended by force of application, we flay the lovely green flesh to leave only intact the vegetal skeleton, the ravishing and delicate framework that makes you think of the skeleton of a sole, which we use to gently caress our arms from elbow to wrist. The road that climbs imperceptibly beneath thick shade finally leads to a little esplanade where the gigantic wings of a windmill turn. The miller of this windmill is also the village mercer and confectioner: he sells cream-filled chocolates, weather vanes, and cotton for mending stockings. Today, he offers us skewers of strange candies, threaded on hazelnut divining rods. The shadows of the mill wings mow down the sun beams on the ground, and the miller-merchant stands worthily before his threshold, very stout, crowned with a Mexican hat so pointed that it resembles a wizard's peaked cap to which the owner has added a broad brim in hopes of protecting his eyes. The miller is named Alcyde, and he is as bandy-legged as my grandmother's coachman. He draws close with a mysterious air of confidentiality, with a wink of the eye, and leaning toward us an unsettling red countenance distorted by uninterrupted laughter, he breathes in our faces:

"They call me Alcyde, but my real name is Cyrille. You had better be careful of Cyrille. He is very dangerous."

And this fat man formed of gold-beater's skin leaves with an elastic step that rebounds from the hardened soil. Having arrived at the base of the mill, he endeavors to climb the steps of his miller's ladder while remaining some distance above the steps, as if more solid steps made of sky and air corresponded to the bars of worm-eaten wood. Finally, he closes the white wooden door to his room behind him, but the wind from the mill wings lifts his straw hat which rolls far from us down the sloping road.

We continue our climb. The opulent trees have given way to scraggy black pines, bristling like the hair of a sleeper who is having a nightmare, and to vast bare meadows that cow dung makes resemble a green fabric strewn with brown discs. Occasionally, the large maternal animals carefully pass their heads through the barriers of brass wire, enfolding me in their reassuring breath, gazing at me with their great vague eyes, redolent of repose and of Asia. We pass by the long white walls of the madhouse: in the courtyard of the hospice, an elderly woman seated in an unyoked carriage unceasingly combs her false hair. I have been a bit uneasy since learning that Cyrille is a dangerous man, but the gaze of my young companion reassures me, and I smile at him in turn with the pathetic smile of children who want to prove that they haven't hurt themselves. I know that the house where I lived as a child elsewhere than in dream is hidden behind this last pine forest, and I explain to my friend that, above all else, we must search out in the linen room a very old wicker mannequin, inside which one could creep when wishing to escape discovery by grownups.

We are a little tired, but I absolutely must show this house to my companion in order to explain to him how unhappy we were there. We go beyond the former stables, where I notice that the swallows' nests are more numerous than ever. The swallows fly very low: by which I mean to say that they fly soundlessly and they fly close to the ground. At the end of an alleyway full of withered rhododendron and dead chrysanthemums, we arrive at what should be the porch with its inevitable geraniums in stone pots. But there are no more geraniums, no more staircases or terraces, no porch, no house. More beautiful still: only trees remain behind, along with the eddy of clouds in the vast gray sky. If I had been awake, I would have remembered that the war had long ago destroyed this house not even the ruins of which belong to me, but the sound of the 1914 bombardments have not yet reached the place where my dream happens. The slanting meadow flies away beneath our gaze, strewn with hazy wreckage and spotted with black places stripped bare by the trail of fire. A few lopped trees, peeled of their bark, reduced to a mere hard trunk, incorruptible as the shafts of columns, remain upright at the emplacement of the forest set ablaze. Like theater set pieces, they restrict the infinity of the landscape, and these tortured silhouettes recall Saint Sebastians, flayed figures of Marsyas, Christs reabsorbed inside the tree that served as their gallows. Beyond the edge of the land where the vanished house once stood, the view spreads out over a landscape where nothing more opposes the profound gray flow; blue smoke rising from aromatic heaps burned in gardens, black smoke emerging from the gullets of factory smoke-stacks expand heavily beneath the low sky where, here and there, the windows of a village church struck by the sun gleam with a metallic brightness like the copper on the keel of a boat. All the way down, guessed rather than discovered behind the unvaryingly lusterless waves of rustic verdure, the sea, provider of clouds and gentle breezes, sends us her deep sigh. The ever stronger whistling of the sea breeze, sharp as the ringing that precedes the departure of a ship, gives notice of the approaching end of my dream, while the two children that we are, holding each other close to withstand the cold wind, finally joining their bare hands, silently consider the empty space before them, astonished and consoled by the immensity.

The Young Girl Who Weeps

I am lodging in a hotel room, lost in the remotest section of an unknown city of immense gray buildings. I share this large room with its faded hangings with the man I once loved. But this arrangement which seems quite natural to us in the dream does not bring us closer together; instead we live as separately as if we inhabited two different countries, or as if one of us were deprived of life. At night, my friend prowls mysterious locales where he is exposed to danger, while I remain seated before the window, its panes worn out by dint of my constant staring. By day, he sleeps, while I come and go in the city, burdened with tasks which replace sleep. We have lost all hope and are very poor. At the beginning of this dream, I am settled in my customary place; I'm darning stockings and the twilight is already well established in the room. A gentle hand knocks at the door. I make out immediately that this cannot be the maid, or my companion since he inevitably slips out the backstairs. I am going to unlock it, after first hiding the torn stockings under the armchair.

A young sixteen-year-old girl is standing on the threshold. She is a young Englishwoman of miraculous beauty, so fragile and so blond that she resembles a moonbeam coifed with sunlight. The epidermis of her face recalls the delicate skin of roses, but she is pale, as if all of her lifeblood has left her heart. She is somewhat breathless since she has run up the stairs and her lips quiver as if she were freezing. She is wearing a thin white muslin dress strewn with little bouquets, far too light for the already advanced season. She takes a seat in the middle of the room in an armchair with long fringe and she searches the twilight:

"He's not here?" She asks.

"No, as you see," I reply. "He never comes back when it snows."

"It is just that I've brought him some flowers," she moans. "Soon they will be all faded . . ."

Indeed, I notice that she is balancing on her knees a risibly small flowerpot containing only two rosebuds, already blighted by frost, that nothing in the world could ever make blossom again. She resumes and I detect the tremor of withheld tears in her voice:

"There is also my letter. I would prefer for him to read it while the ink is still very fresh."

And she takes out of her bodice a little envelope folded in two. I place the rose on the eiderdown quilt over the bed, where men's clothing is flung in disorder, and I pin the letter to the edge of the pillow. A meek smile springs up in the young girl's childish face. She docilely arranges the large straw hat that she had taken off before entering the room and, using its ribbon, she wipes away the tears which continue to stream, as if she knew in the depths of her heart that no trace of hope remained for her. She turns back once more to smile at me from the threshold, but I know that her tears will stream again as soon as the door is closed.

The man whom we love comes in almost at once and I am surprised that he hadn't met the young girl on the landing. Perhaps he didn't notice her: she was so piteous. His hands singed with cold and his face evenly white beneath his green felt hat resemble the face and hands of a frozen man living within an iceberg. The moment he notices the rose and letter pinned to the bed, he is beset with silent rage, like several degrees of a more intense cold capable of burning. The rage which mottles his face aggravates the green shadows around his eyes. He feverishly rips the little envelope and the buds of dead roses, and the white shreds scatter through the room, drifting snowflakes undecided where to rest. He picks up the telephone receiver and gets ready to lie the way a virtuoso prepares to play. He explains to the absent young girl that he hadn't returned, that he no longer lives in this city, that he hasn't received her letter and wants nothing to do with her flowers. At the other end of the receiver, the young girl weeps so loudly that she is heard throughout the room, and the man whom she has hopelessly loved begins to smile an insolent smile worse than hatred, just as her own smile was worse than anguish.

The second part of my dream begins in the street. It remains or is once again night. It is not snowing: it is drizzling lightly and I am trudging through the filthy mire of the thaw. Across from the building where I live, a private mansion raises the three floors of its gray facade; only the windows of the ground floor are illuminated; they have neither curtains nor shutters, and my gaze penetrates the interior of the house through the bare panes. The insane young girl from a moment ago is standing in the middle of a vast unfurnished salon: she has taken down two crystal chandeliers where several dozen candles blaze with myriad fire, and she dances, at first languidly, then faster and faster, to the point of breathlessness, holding at arm's length the two chandeliers, melodiously dashing against each other their crystalline stalactites. I know that she dances with anguish as others dance with joy. Her flexible throat falls back on her shoulders, allowing a face, as sweet and ravaged as a rose battered by wind, to roll in abandon. The bright fire of the candles spreads to the flounces of her muslin dress which begins to burn with a beautiful flame, even and pure, but it seems that anguish or the dance have robbed her of all sense of danger for she is no more worried about her dress caught on fire than if she were already dead and her blazing dress enveloped nothing more than her soul. While dancing, she incessantly weeps, and her tears scatter around her with the droplets of scorching wax.

I cannot allow the young girl to whirl round in the flame; I sense that I must, come what may, inform the man whom we love, since only he is capable of stopping this dance of death, of fire and crystal. But I don't know where to find him, in what corner of this vast somber city. Swept away by the slope of the streets, I heedlessly descend toward the river. At times, I slip on the ice, at times, I sink in heavy dark mud. Rare passers-by prowl along the gloomy lanes; gradually, as I wander through more and more wasted neighborhoods, the silhouettes which come and go in the mist, beneath the vitreous gaze of the streetlamps, turn leaner and more gray: green faces, like those of the drowned, float in the thickened atmosphere; malice, meanness, coarse hypocrisy flower upon their cheeks like an eczema brought on by misery and misfortune; and their voices resemble the rasping of a file on iron or shattering glass. By degrees, the streets grow empty, as if I walked in a city decimated by typhus or flu; in this solitude, you can hear the foul and pestilential plashing of the water of the river. Not far from the wharf, on the threshold of a brothel, I finally encounter the one I have sought, but I find him again only to realize that he is irrevocably lost to both of us women. These are indeed his clothes, but worn thin and threadbare, as if we had been separated not since the day before but for years, for all time; this is indeed his face but pale and spoiled like that of a dead man who no longer expects any help. He is tired, as if he hadn't slept since the first night of creation, and he gives in to this exhaustion, this sorrow because he is alone. Standing in the doorway, he nervously wraps a scarf of garnet red wool around his neck and he gets ready to plunge into the mist and the empty streets. A thick crust of despair overlays his features, his mouth, leaving only a little of his eyes exposed. The fate of the young girl in flames disappears into the background, as if his masculine affliction were the only one worthy of pity; I do not, however, dare draw near him; I consider his solitude as a form of nudity that I have no right to spy on in secret; yet, I would sacrifice the little I have if only I could place my hands on his temples and remove this face the way you lift off a mask.

Love and the Linen Shroud

I am in a room, at a bedside, with the man I love. I am stretched out in the bed, overwhelmed by the mesmerized animal quivering that lays hold of women in the presence of love. We had just attended the performance of a traveling circus, its raucous music prolonged in a stertorous moan beneath our open windows. We went out before the end of the show, leaving a pair of clowns to grasp each other's long blond mops. It was raining: my drenched clothes are strewn over the parquet and my damp shoes are there, still warm from having been worn. Suddenly, the wheezing music comes to a stop, replaced by the numberless trampling of a crowd flowing out of the doors of painted canvas down below; the thousands of deadened footsteps, as if muffled by felt slippers, resound indistinctly in the street, now nothing more than a large shining pool. Then the darkness lowers like the shutter on a window; the streetlamps are extinguished, and I have only a patch of black sky before my eyes. But a small electric lamp burns at the head of the bed. My companion stretches out his arm, as if to brush aside or point out something, and his gesture displaces and causes the light to flicker, as if it were a candle flame. Only then do I discover that my friend is not, in the strictest sense of the word, clothed but only wrapped up in countless little bands, a sort of mummified Apollo. The thin tightly pressed cloths, like those of the Egyptian dead or the leggings of soldiers or racing cyclists, are entirely covered with black serried marks suggestive of the print in a book of magic spells, and this profusion of indecipherable letters recalls the spirals of newspaper which were used to enfold our legs as children, to keep us warm. Gradually, as my companion undresses, or rather patiently unrolls the interminable bands which intersect in all directions over his body, the dimly lit floor is covered with a heap not unlike the dressings strewn about the bedside of the wounded. At last, however, he grows tired of this drawn-out, complicated unwinding and is satisfied from this point on with vigorously rubbing his arms, chest, thighs; clearing away, with broad sweeps of his hand, the thick soft pulp which is destroyed like the diseased paper of old posters or pieces of newsprint dampened from having been pressed to the stems of flower bouquets. This simple rubbing suffices to remove all trace of humanity, as well as the clothing, from this compact and firm body, restoring its shape and godlike nudity. He stretches out over me with the unconcern of a tired man lying down in bed; between my arms and between my knees, I press this body more loved than God, more essential than my own life, and such is the unspeakable excess of my happiness that I awaken (this being, no doubt, the only way of losing consciousness in a dream).

Posthumous Materials

File on Dreams and Destinies

[The following file, based upon that provided in volume II, *Essays and Memoires,* of Marguerite Yourcenar's complete works in the Pléiade Edition, reflects the author's intention of revising and expanding the preface of the 1938 edition of *Dreams and Destinies,* as well as of supplementing the original narrations with a later group of commented dreams. The texts are found in documentation housed in the Archives of the Editions Gallimard, Paris, and also, where indicated, in additional documents in "Sources II, Meditations and Dreams" from the Marguerite Yourcenar collection at the Houghton Library, Harvard University, shelf mark bMS FR372.2. All bracketed commentary on the following pages summarizes the remarks of the Pléiade editorial group in compiling the documentation.]

Quotations for Dreams and Destinies

[In accordance with the author's wish, extracts from *The Memoirs of Hadrian* and *The Abyss* were provided as epigraphs, alongside the quotation from Heraclitus which established the mood of the original edition. The use of the following quotations on typed leaves, one unnumbered and the others paginated 1-4, was not specified by the author.]

"Sleep is the digestion of sensory impressions. Dreams are excretions."

Novalis, from J. C. Schneider's French translation in
Cahiers du Sud, no. 331, 1965

"A tale is incoherent as a dream; it is a harmony of whatever exists and wondrous events, a musical imagination [. . .], nature itself. Nothing is as contrary to the spirit of the tale as a didactic necessity, as a coherence prescribed by laws. The tale is the anarchy of nature, an abstract world, oneiric. From this abstraction, we are to draw certain conclusions regarding our state after death."

Novalis, same source

"Let us consider them well, these *Prisons* which are, along with Goya's *Black Paintings,* one of the most secret works bequeathed to us by a man of the eighteenth century. From the very first, it is clear that a dream is at issue. No connoisseur of oneiric subject matter would hesitate for a moment when faced with these pages marked with all of the essential characteristics of the dream state: the negation of time, the displacement of space, suggested levitation, the rapture of reconciling or rising above the impossible, a dread that is nearer to ecstasy than is realized by those who analyze the visionary's production from the outside, the absence of connection or visible contact between the portions or the dramatis personae of the dream, and, finally, the fatal, ineluctable beauty."

The Dark Brain of Piranesi
Marguerite Yourcenar, 1961

Notes on Dreams

[These notes are typed on eight leaves paginated from 5-12, following the quotations. They are without correction in the author's hand. Along with manuscript notes that follow and from which these are perhaps extracted, the notes may constitute a preliminary stage for recasting the preface to *Dreams and Destinies*.]

Art and poetry are like the beautiful sequences of the dream, in that we detach them from the whole in order to isolate them more or less consciously in our memory. Reality resembles the dream in its entirety.

The soul always chooses.

It is by force of habit that life appears less *absurd* to us than the dream.

Every dream is infinitely more complex than its analysts and commentators assume. It remains a piquant spectacle to observe the human understanding drain a subject, be it dream or fact, of three quarters of its contents before settling in to study it by the smoking light of a theory or hypothesis.

Open the paltry *Keys to Dreams* that date from the nineteenth century and whose volumes with gaudy covers are still occasionally found in the boxes of secondhand book dealers. You will doubtlessly share my surprise at not having encountered in those humble dictionaries a single oneiric combination that you have actually dreamed. All of those marriages that mean "death," all of those deaths that mean "marriage," all of those blond women in black dresses and those brunettes in white dresses, those visits to the dentist and biting dogs never belonged to the vocabulary of our dreams. Might differences in dream exist not only

between epochs but between social classes as well? Here is something
disconcerting yet stimulating to our *dreaming* meditation.

Even our most individual dreams are still crammed with social,
ethnic, and historical elements. Oneiric themes vary from epoch to
epoch, just as philosophies, clothing styles, and culinary trends
appear to obey the strange law which demands that within almost
closed circuits the human spirit refines, combines, repeats, compli-
cates, reorganizes, and unmakes purely experimental and purely
speculative constructions, as remote as possible from the plausible
and the real. Even the great archetypal dreams isolated by Jung cannot
escape disguise by prevailing fashion. Those oracular visions dreamed
by the Greeks at the foot of Aesculapius's statue, within the precincts
of sacred dormitories, *The Dream of Poliphili* replete with the spirit of
a voluptuous and chimerical Renaissance, those of German romanticism where shadows and lights flicker disquietingly are as much a
product of a given time and place as no matter what tangible and
visible production of the period. The dreams gathered by Artemi-
dorus in the second century of our era give the impression of sites
once frequently visited, but where no one goes any longer. The
dreams deciphered on Assyrian tablets leave the reader with a sense
of uneasiness: visions foreign to us that unfold according to rhythms
which are not our own; even more so than the documentation of the
waking state found alongside them in the same archeological digs, the
dream transcriptions reveal to us the beating pulse of a so-called
barbarous civilization. The majority of dreams collected and anno-
tated by psychoanalysts will, no doubt, also produce this sensation of
obsolescence. It is most assuredly natural, and unavoidable, that the
pressure of time molds our dreams and that the great primordial
dreams which haunt us change aspect from generation to generation
like the Venuses and the Marys of the altars. It is rather the variations

in dream combinations from epoch to epoch that throw our minds into confusion and cause us to doubt, by analogy, our diurnal mental constructions.

One wonders with stupefaction how certain psychologists could claim that we always dream in black and white. A good number of the people I have questioned dream in color. In my own experience, the chromatic element is perhaps the most significant component of a dream.

Above all, the chromatic element is significant in its intensity. Words are lacking to convey the depth, the suavity, the radiance, the refulgence or somber violence of the color of far reaches of sky, of vast natural formations, plains, oceans, or mountains, and occasionally, though much less frequently, of buildings, accessories, or clothing. Vivifying colors that make you dance with joy and some that constrict your heart with their beauty. It is through the intensity and modulation of color that we are able to recognize what I call, for want of a better term, the great dreams.

Man has long endeavored in vain to establish a symbology of color. Rimbaud's is not mine and is probably not yours either. Nor does the medieval illuminator's concur with the Chinese symbolist's. Freud insisted strongly on the color white, symbol of virginity, and he is probably correct when he interprets dreams of nineteenth-century Vienna, in a time and a place where both the sensibility and eroticism insisted strongly on the white of wedding gowns. But Renaissance brides willingly chose to be married in red, as is the case in the Orient. Inert and leaden color, white for the Chinese is a symbol of mourning and, similarly, it is the color of death and ghosts in medieval legends and in our dreams. For an alchemist, white is, on the contrary, the color of the Great Work that follows the calcinations of black and prepares us for the splendors of red: it is the already subtle and almost disembodied state of a substance on the way to transmutation. This incandescent and almost excessive white also occurs sometimes in dreams. Red is even more subject to contradiction. Color of joy for the oriental; color associated with beauty for the Slav, which makes Red Square in Moscow the Beautiful Square for the Russian imagination; while the same word for the westerner immediately conjures the sinister flow from executions. The nomenclator's naiveté consists in not taking into account the *diapason* of colors, the immense distance that separates, emotionally and chromatically, two nuances thought to be proximate. There is red and red, white and white. Also to be taken into consideration is the sleeper's share of inexplicable liberty, as he selects, rejects, or transforms a color without even realizing it, just as he chooses without realizing it among his phantasms, the decision invariably the result of a series of immediate or far-flung reasons, of which we at most glimpse but a few. All of the books and the entire universe could be exhausted without discovering exactly why Fra Angelico employed a certain red, its like found nowhere else, for the gowns of his saints and angels, or why Correggio so often painted in mauve. And yet, we certainly feel that these colors provide us with instruction about the composition of a soul, just as spectrum analysis does about that of the stars. Mankind dwells somewhere in the midst of the prism.

If I attempt to establish a list of the colors in my own dreams, the predominant is perhaps rose, a marvelous rose color that flows from the flower of that name to the nuance of the most lovely of rose evenings; a deep blue, suave, polished, gently blending other shades of blue into itself, like water seen through water: at first a very dense blue, almost black, but strewn with light like the night with stars, or allowing these to be divined behind its darkness, then a very rich and soft blue, belonging rather to the scale of colors invented by man than to that of natural objects, and which most closely approximates the serene blue of the cloaks of French kings in certain medieval illuminations. Then an extraordinarily young and tender green, often as pale as the first leaves, and, like grass, seemingly capable of infinite expansion. A white, almost always of snow, unless it is applied to certain faces when it turns marmorean. These four colors, to which it would be necessary to add, although much more rarely visible, a certain sandy *blond* always associated with the idea of a plain beneath the sunlight, appear to be the only ones susceptible of covering immense spaces in my dreams, of conveying the impression of dreaming in blue, in green, or in blond. The role of black is more limited, figuring especially in the guise of interior night, within rooms and underground passages, more or less linked with an impression of descent into the underworld; it is rarely worn by characters in the dream. There is also the black of certain animals' coats, likewise intensely felt as "awe inspiring." Red appears so infrequently that I have trouble finding an example, and it usually is manifest at the extreme limit of rose, at the moment when it turns to carmine. Brown and gray do not appear as colors properly so-called but as a veneering, perceived to varying degrees, of buildings and rocks. Almost always whenever buildings or rocks reach a certain visionary intensity, they veer to black, blond, or to the ardent rose of which I spoke above. As far as I recall, no violet, no orange, no silver, and no gold.

In order to avoid misunderstandings, let us immediately assert that this oneiric chromatic scale in no way corresponds to the taste in color that I manifest in life. I am partial to black clothes. I enjoy wearing and gazing upon gold and silver rings against the gray-brown of my fingers, and, just as much as the ineffable rose color of roses, I never grow weary of the sumptuous and sober violet of irises and hyacinths. This false notion must be consistently rebuked, namely that we dream about our preferences.

The more highly colored a dream is, the more unforgettable. In certain dreams, an inexplicable happiness is born from the effect of two or three brilliantly colored cloths flapping in the wind. A rose sky seen in a dream is evidently the chromatic equivalent of eternal bliss.

Expanses in dream: the sacred beauty and the delight of dream derives in great part from that dilation of the sense of space, majesty of architecture, mass and height of rocks, but especially the almost infinite lengthening of terrestrial or marine perspectives. Just as the dreamer walks tirelessly, the immensity of space is never accompanied by feelings of apprehension or discouragement before these solitary reaches too vast ever to be crossed or objects too distant ever to be easily reached. Even in nightmares in which one strays interminably through dark corridors or flees assassins from street to street, the anguish is never accompanied by weariness. Even the most ridiculous dreams (for one is also frequently ridiculous in dream)—uninteresting visits with friends or acquaintances, buying newspapers, meeting the mailman, or paying a bill at the grocer's—sometimes grow beautiful and sacrosanct with the immensity of the background perceived here and there through the interstices of the banal human anecdote. Even in the greatest dreams, the intrigue counts less than certain dimensions of the earth and sky.

Notes Intended for Addition to the Preface

[These notes are preserved as an autographic manuscript, written on 22 leaves paginated I-III and 8-30. Several leaves are missing and may have been removed from the manuscript after the preceding "Notes on Dreams" had been typed.]

These notes are intended for addition to the preface of *Dreams and Destinies.* At the time when I first set down the series of dreams that comprise this book I was still hesitant about overtly mingling scientific or philosophical reflection on the phenomena of dream with the literary transcription of the dream experience. As a result, the absolutely authentic transcriptions contained in *Dreams and Destinies* could, at first glance, strike the uninitiated reader as simple tales or as prose poems, *imitating* the processes of dream and not as what they really are, the statement of authenticated nocturnal adventures.

The fear of falling into pedantry or pseudoscience was not the only decisive factor. The dreams reported in *Dreams and Destinies,* almost all quite proximate in *nocturnal time,* are set inside a moment of my life completely obsessed with an intense and violent love. It would have been impossible for me to have made an attempt at establishing a key to these dreams without indiscretion toward myself and others. At twenty years' distance, this danger has almost disappeared.

Surrealism was engrossed in the dream. Not very advantageously, at least in my opinion. Namely, a poet like Breton chose to worship the dream almost superstitiously, almost mystically, if you would, to honor it for its confusions, its mysteries, its dark night, an absurdity even more profound than that of life itself, to be its adherent and not its explorer, the Vasco da Gama or Columbus of dream, who is even now lacking and who someday will prepare the map of these nocturnal regions. For surrealism, the dream has become *(horresco referens!)* a literary genre, and the oneiric symbols a part of the trappings of the school, not unlike ravenous dogs for Racine's imitators.

Proust, who has so admirably expressed himself on the nature of sleep, has but rarely, and poorly, expressed himself on dream. He only perceived its far fetched absurdity and the distorted continuation (like the images of a partially immersed object) of the day's anxieties. (Saint-Loup's dream about his mistress; Marcel's dream about Mme. Verdurin; Swann's dream.) No analysis of dreams matches in depth those that he undertook more than once of the diverse orders of sleep.

> *Tremble, she proclaimed, wretched daughter most worthy of me!*
> *The vengeful God of the Jews will vanquish you as well,*
> *How I weep as you fall into His terrible hands,*
> *My daughter. . . .*

Does logical, articulated language function in dream? This passage from Athalie's vision in sleep belongs rather to the traditional genre of recounting a ghostly visitation than to dream. In my own experience and in that of the few individuals whom I have questioned, the vast majority of dreams are voiceless, or if room for organized language exists, it is limited to a few exclamations or to extremely brief phrases, sibylline and oracular at times, striking in their very rarity, without our ever being able to remember, for example, the various replies in a dialogue or reproduce the articulations of a discourse. The exception is a peculiar type of dream, infrequently described, wherein the word, on the contrary, abounds, and almost always in the form of a monologue: the ratiocinating dream to which I will return.

Apparently, one of the essential qualities of the dream is the inability or extreme difficulty we have in remembering it. It seems that the majority of people forget their dreams at most some few hours after awakening and, furthermore, in most cases, they preserve upon awakening only some scattered and confused fragments, trifling in respect to the totality of the dream, or even just a vague impression, agreeable or unpleasant, without imagistic accompaniment whatsoever. Even the experimenter who has assiduously trained himself to remember his dreams never has the impression of having completely avoided all omission. But it has not been sufficiently observed that this rapid, total, or partial forgetfulness also governs what I would label the imaginative vision in all of its forms.

The writer who prepares a literary work by telling it to himself or by allowing his narration to unfold without intervention before him, without writing or taking notes of any sort benefits from a sort of induced vision analogous to the dream insofar as it is devoid of effort, relatively devoid of critical controls (the author having *voluntarily* eliminated these), and also in that it unfolds like a dream within a purely imaginary time. The visions of the work that precede and prepare the work itself often bestow upon the author a dazzled amazement and joy equal to that brought by the most beautiful dreams and *of the same nature,* which the finished piece of work certainly does not always procure for him. But this creative vision, precisely like the dream, is exposed to a prompt and almost total [forgetfulness]: it suffices for this almost perfect development of images to be interrupted for a *few seconds* and an entire hour of imaginative construction crashes again into oblivion. Even more, the writer instinctively senses that he must avoid forcing his memory, that it is better for him to await another occasion for silent reflection in order to allow this film to somehow pass for a second and then a third time beneath his gaze, until the day comes when a series of images, somehow learned by heart, will be retained and recalled at will by the voluntary memory. The dreamer is denied this faculty of somehow being able to play back his dream. But what I find significant in both cases is the incredible volatility of the memory in contrast to the extraordinary intensity of the impression.

Upon careful consideration, the same occurs, though on an infinitely more superficial level, in the case of what I would label the

artificial vision, offered from the outside and intended to rouse and
excite the imagination without overlapping our everyday lives. The
amateur of middle-of-the-road culture, untrained in critical faculty,
who is deeply moved by a television performance or a play or, yet again,
is dazzled by an exhibition of paintings or a single visit to a museum,
comes out believing himself in possession of an enduring memory, but
how swiftly the details blur, the subject and the plot twists of the play
fall into oblivion, the names of the painters appearing in the exhibition,
the arrangement of the paintings and their systems of lines and color
strokes evanesce, and nothing remains of the play apart from that "blond
who wept so well on the sofa, wearing a green dress," or "that landscape
with rocks in the background, wonderful. . . ." The passive artistic
vision, which for a moment lifted the individual outside himself, ends
by being limited to a few images, a few symbols emerging from
forgetfulness like those of a dream.

Let us pursue our comparison no further than in what seems to be
the most solid domain of memory, that of facts, in what could be
labeled the vision of lived reality. Here as well, the facts that we *behold*
again are fragmentary, thrilling, standing out sharply against a
background of forgetfulness or against the lusterless fabric of facts
that we have recalled as a bloodless, skeletal nomenclature, but
without *experiencing them,* without *beholding them again.* Let us produce one or two more recent examples than those I discussed at the
end of the 1936 preface to *Dreams and Destinies,* in which I had already
reached the same conclusions.

In 1939, at the end of September or the beginning of October, passing
through Ouchy, I went to Lausanne to bid farewell to Edmond Jaloux
before my departure for the United States. We spent the evening together:
there was a private dinner at the Hotel Central, the details of which have
slipped my memory, and a conversation, of which nothing remains with

me. But I behold again, sharply defined and indelible, the image of Edmond Jaloux pacing the deserted and darkened place Saint-François, abandoned to the blackout, waiting for the last bus that was coming to take me away. The slightest detail of his apparel, his cape, his stick, his weighted silhouette at once soft and massive, his somewhat yellow face, impenetrable even in sadness (I was never to see him again) have remained forever fixed in my memory, as well as the blackened and somewhat provincial portal of the church, the sleeping pigeons, the heavy facade of a banking house, the supple and soundless approach of the bus that took me away, inside which the only passenger, a disheveled and forward Waldensian vine grower, leaned close to me to ask at all hazards whether I were not "young Mme. Dubois?" With this fragment of reality, precise down to the smallest detail and following the simple process that consists of isolating it from the rest, memory has fabricated the equivalent of a dream.

My other example is drawn from the days and nights of Paris in time of war (of that strange war), about a month after the preceding memory. Of that anxious, weighted, almost suffocating period, I find again neither the hurried errands to the offices nor those to the banks, nothing of the two overwhelming personal concerns, visas and money, and also nothing of the enormous political preoccupation of that time, to the extent that if there were no contemporary history books at my disposal allowing me to correct the dates, I would readily believe that troops had already landed in Norway during that cold autumn or that in Paris, already three-quarters decimated, the June exodus had taken place seven months too early.

The recollections that I have kept and that I note here in the order that they rise to the surface of memory are of the deserted streets at night, gleaming with a moonlight no longer marred by a single streetlamp, and where two individuals, N. C. and myself, advanced "as if in dream." There are the immense spaces of the Concorde without traffic, the arcades of the rue de Rivoli stretching endlessly, the hollow star of the place Vendome with all signal lights extinguished, and, in the pale, lunar blue, the column that simultaneously conjures dreams of the magnificence of imperial Rome and of the curious, lewd designs of a nineteenth-century eroticism:

> *Bereaved of her . . . the Glory*
> *Sunken in her . . . sovereign*
> *Every night . . .*

And indeed the nocturnal city looked as if it were given over to the illusory, immersed in an almost demented reverie, appeared to be the wraithlike semblance of an already long defunct Rome, revived by the magic spell of an enchanter or a poet and frozen in a motionless duration that is no longer time. And next to these gigantic Chiricos improvised by the war, the recollection of genuine Chiricos at a friend's, of a red leather armchair, and of Julien Gracq in uniform, standing in a corner of the drawing room. And then, a new raincoat; a hole where I stumbled while wandering the streets one moonless night and lost a shoe that I could only find again the next day; a humpbacked cashier, her cheeks enflamed with rouge, who preferred women; S. with his moving tales that decisively colored my judgments about F.; Jean Cocteau at the Ritz—the black eye and the elongate bone-thin, agile hands—complaining that I had too cavalierly introduced his name into a book; an old shoemaker alone in his shop, his wife and children fled to the countryside, but convinced that Hitler couldn't be such a bad man since he was put in charge of his country; a Hawaiian record on which was moaned the most astonishing amorous plaint I ever heard; B. L. lost in the pitch-black night at the door to a cafe; a defective phone call and, at the other end of the wire, cawing like a crow, a voice once loved; a brief alarm and my going down into the street during the early hours, heading for the nearest shelter in a violet dressing gown as incongruous in that setting as the strange or scanty clothes paraded "in dream." How is it possible not to realize that these recollections that rise to the surface almost automatically have the incoherent, incongruous, absurd futility, and also the obsessive intensity of those of dream, with their appearance of having come from another world where everything is more significant and stands out with greater beauty than in our own? By the simple process invoked by writer and artist and which consists of dropping the dull, insignificant, or gray detail, the involuntary memory has built from authentic facts the same type of edifice that the dreaming man builds with an admixture of [lacuna] dream visions and wherein the primitive man discovers his dead. Furthermore, the most striking images that the poets and theologians have given us of "the other world"—Homer's Hades, Virgil's Elysian Fields, Dante's Hell, the Egyptian and Tibetan books of the dead—resemble the convolutions of dream to the point of mistaken identity. We might conclude by positing the existence of a vast, partially fluid universe where the individual would drift from symbols to symbols, from transforma-tions to transformations, and from which we might have only momentary opportunities for escape through our intelligence, logical reason, quan-titative evaluation, disinterested discernment, all of the faculties that are offered and lent to us in the course of a life but of which we do not always avail ourselves. And thus we would conclude that the side of life governed by the intelligence is the adventitious exception, a unique privilege strictly limited for each of us in time and space, within a human universe almost entirely given over to the shadowy approximations of dreams.

Dream: world where everything, even terror, is implicitly *accepted*— world of conflict and not of antagonism. As far as I know, one has never experienced a quarrel in dream.

Dream: *world of aspiration and project,* world of terror, anxiety, aston-ishment, of the pursuit of desire, of expectation rather than fulfillment

(the two sole exceptions being the erotic orgasm and mystic delectation, of which more later); world whose most frequent aspect is that
of the journey, the quest, of displacement from one point to another.
The dream as a rudimentary form of investigation.

I do not eat in dream. But the dreams in which you see, buy,
prepare, or offer food are not rare.

I do not believe that I have experienced actual physical pain in dream.
Even in the nightmare with its predominant apprehension and terror,
the horror never reaches the expected result of pain. Awakening usually
takes place before the pursuing murderer kills you; in the sole instance
in which I am dead and the dream has extended after my death, the
allegorical passage did not give rise to the least suffering. I also never
suffered from wounds inflicted on me or blows I have met with. The
dreams of illness (I think particularly of dreams of the type ["The Woman
Stricken with Leprosy"] that I have often dreamed again with variations
since the time when I have [lacuna] neither sleep nor dream, but
nonetheless culminating at the very extreme point of amorous pleasure
which oneiric eroticism has offered many times. I would not emphasize
this if I did not find it remarkable that in the world of dream, where
anguish and terror usually stop on this side of the pain that they seem to
predict, pleasure on the contrary flourishes with such facility that it
seems to race ahead without stopping for the stage of desire. I remember
having experienced pleasure but not having desired in dream.

Clearly impossible to prove that this amorous pleasure experienced in
dream is not the simple reflection of a physical pleasure actually experienced during sleep, a couple's pleasure if the sleep takes place in a shared
bed, in other cases, a solitary pleasure born of a position that mechanically
induces sensuality. Imperfect explanation, precisely because it leaves aside
the salient fact: the pleasure, whether it be half-real or purely oneiric, is

fulfilled within a dream without interrupting it and without leading to awakening, whereas real pain felt by the dreamer consistently awakens him and the fear of imaginary pain is usually sufficient to do the same.

Would it not then be necessary to conclude that pain possesses an absolute value, an exponential power that pleasure, in spite of everything, is lacking?

Kinsey, if I am not mistaken, wrote somewhere that we cannot understand and classify the erotic comportment of men and women with the aid of the waking dream: they act in one way and often fantasize in another. One can also not deduce the dreamer's erotic propensities from the dream, properly so-called. With respect to myself, I can verify that my preferences and choices in matters of partners and amorous play take up little room in the eroticism of my dreams. The facility that reigns in dreams is such that I have tasted in them, often with beings whom I would have overlooked in life, pleasures that take no account of the gender and very little account of the willingness or beauty of the partners, but which is almost invariably reduced to the *most basic*. In diametric opposition to the almost fabulous phantasmagoria of the waking dream, the dream per se seems to ignore the wonderful feats and the expert recipes of the erotologists.

"Nothing in the mind that was not first perceived through the intermediary of the senses." In dream, this is true for me in everything concerning the erotic, *but only the erotic*. It has never come to pass that I experienced a voluptuous sensation in dream that I hadn't first [felt] in reality. On the contrary, other notions of velocity, soaring on high, vast reaches, coloration frequently surpass for me, both in variety and intensity, impressions in the waking state. Therefore, these especially constitute the grace of dreams.

I label erotic dreams all in which the voluptuous sensation contin-ues to the point of orgasm. Some statistical analysis may not be amiss—This type of dream never constituted for me more than 7-8% of the whole of visionary dreams.

If I insist in this way, it is because the erotic dream, properly so-called, happens to be so frequently left out of accounts of dreams. The Freudian analysts with their pansexual theory perceived eroticism everywhere, in larvated or latent form, but seldom signaled it in its complete development where it actually exists. It seems that the patients whose narrations of dreams they elucidated must all have been subject to a censorship carried out on the verbal level or, more profoundly, within the dream itself. It is curious, it is almost extraordinary that Freudianism perhaps [lacuna].

Freudianism believed too strongly in the irremovability of the symbol.

It is not true that symbols are necessarily connected. One could think of an obelisk, sundial, without thinking or implying on an unconscious level, obelisk, phallic symbol. One may think of the cat, symbol of the night, without thinking of the cat, symbol of the female organ, or more particularly of its hair. The feline could also become the symbol of suppleness, masculine and savage strength, of danger, cunning, clean-liness, domestic comfort, maliciousness, ferocity. The symbol will play itself out differently if the dreamer is an animal lover or scorns them, collects stray cats or raises birds. In the final analysis, it is not the symbol that will instruct us about man's secrets, but what we know about the man that determines the meaning of the symbol.

Freudianism believed too strongly in the unity of the symbol.

Freudianism did not sufficiently perceive the metaphoric component of the symbol, its purely aesthetic play. It tends to attribute an obsessive intensity to the symbol which this does not always possess.

That the serpent may be capable of serving as a phallic symbol, no one doubts, as well as a symbol of vigilance, of wisdom, of divine contact with mother earth through its creeping, of eternity through its coils. But all of these symbols especially pertain to the ancient consciousness or unconsciousness. (Ancient and pre-Christian, not oriental and Mediterranean in opposition to western, for the Scandinavian sagas of the pagan period also do not express horror of the serpent, quite the reverse.) That the Christian populations, simultaneously inculcated with the notion of carnal guilt, are the only ones in which hatred and terror of the reptile have taken on an instinctual character, superstitious, hysterical, and almost sacred, causes us to reflect and would permit us to wonder whether it is not in the guise of a sexual symbol that the serpent was adopted by the Christian consciousness as a symbol of evil, and whether the image of the Virgin felling the serpent is not, after all, the simplest and most complete allegorical image formed by the Christian anti-erotic, a sort of idealized, mass-produced image of the struggle against the sin of sexuality.

The question grows most singularly entangled through the simple fact that the snake is, in truth, a dangerous animal, at least with regard to certain representatives of the species, and that the quasi impossibility of immediately recognizing whether or not a poisonous variety is in question makes us surround the majority of reptiles with an aura of legitimate terror. Paradoxically, this is especially true of the populations of European regions where the poisonous snake is relatively rare, and where habit has not blunted the feeling of danger, to which the American Indian, in frequent contact with the terrible rattlesnake, appears, for example, completely indifferent. If fear of snakes were really always linked to an anxiety or repression of a sexual order, it is hard to see how this could coincide for certain people with acceptance and easy affection for these same things. For an amorous woman, it is not the serpent, an often noxious animal, that is the consummate sexual metaphor, but the flowering branch, the mast dressed with flags, or yet again, and of a different order, the child which blends the idea of pleasure with that of maternal tenderness, the sword of battles. The erotic song in which Jesus Christ raises his head and enters paradise is only blasphemous for those men or women who have no sense of the sacred in love. It rather evokes the delights of love than [unfinished or unjoined text; on the bottom, right-hand side of the leaf, the following list of titles can be read:]

> *Revue d'histoire des sciences*. Presses universitaires de France, I, place
> Paul-Painlevé, Paris, 1200 F per year for four issues.
> Books to purchase: L. Bourgey. *L'Observation et l'Expérience chez*
> *Aristote*. Urin, 1955.
> M. Renucci. *L'Aventure de l'humanisme européen au Moyen Age*. Les
> Belles Lettres, 1953.
> A. Reymond. *Histoire des Sciences exactes et naturelles dans l'Antiquité*.
> Presses universitaires de France, 1955.

The dreamer's security, even in the midst of danger, the danger being in dream an accepted part of the game, and vaguely experienced as such. Security in the midst of those architectures or those gigantic landscapes that would crush us in the waking state and which do, indeed, overwhelm us whenever we encounter them in the sites of reality through the oppressive sensation of *feeling oneself in a dream*. Security in the presence of the unforeseen, grotesque, or tragic, calmly accepted as such. No state that provides a more expansive impression of being rid of all the accustomed servitudes. The liberated sleeper advances without the least effort in a world at once more fluid and denser than our own, and his very terrors are not our fears.

The absence of vertigo follows. As for me, who suffers and especially suffered excessively from vertigo while awake, I am able at night to lean over no matter what chasm or look down from no matter what height. I will not fall or will fall without being broken.

Oneiric levitation has been one of the most frequently discussed aspects of the dream. It is not separable from the other changes in spatial conditions which I have already mentioned. The sexual explanation of the levitation dream is tempting for self-evident reasons. Analogies, nonetheless, perhaps more metaphorical than real. Nothing in the effortless movement, the gentle, continuous hovering of oneiric levitation recalls the bounding fits and starts, the effort, the throbbing tightening of desire. This nimble world of lightness, at ease in the impalpable, seems to have nothing at all in common with the quite different delights of the world of the flesh.

Zoology of my dreams: the horse, the dog, the bird. More rarely the cat. Always beneficent. Especially the horse charged with a mythological splendor, vigor, bounding energy, in no manner frightening but "awe inspiring," and almost always found in an untrammeled state, careening at a gallop. The birds filled with a sort of tender and enchanted sweetness, leavening, palpitation of life itself; the dogs, like all the dogs one has had [two illegible words] mythological, marvelously free, simple and beautiful. It is with greater surprise that I note the absence of other beloved animals: the wild beasts, whose image and reality haunt me in [unfinished]

The white radiance of eternity (Shelley).

> The poet and the dreamer are distinct,
> Diverse, sheer opposites, antipodes,

The one pours out a balm upon the world,

The other vexes it.

> Keats. *The Fall of Hyperion.* [from a French para-
> phrase in Dubos's *Qu'est-ce la littérature?*]

I have never been convinced by the psychologists who assert that one always dreams and in each and every sleep. Instead, I believe in the existence of admirable slumbers, opaque and dense, in which the dream does not enter.

This inexplicable and essential assertion remains valid for me: concerning myself (and it cannot be overemphasized that the experience of one person only is in question here), the images of the creative imagination are never mingled with dream images. Divergent worlds, separated by airtight partitions. I have never chanced to dream of a single character in my books, even those who preoccupied me for years on end and with whom I lived on the most intimate terms. When most infrequently I do chance to dream of one of my books (and I mean by that one of my books as an actual material object), it is as if I were dreaming of any ordinary, familiar object, some suitcase or kitchen utensil. And neither has it ever come to pass that I have consciously introduced an image taken from a dream into a book.

The most fertile periods of literary activity correspond, on the other hand (and this contradicts every theory of supposed sublimation), with the periods of maximum sensual intensity.[*] Yet, I cannot succeed in

---

[*] This to the extent that I have often asked myself whether sexual activity were not a precondition for literary effort and whether it would be possible to continue this in a period when sensuality is extinguished. I am beginning to understand that sensuality is not extinguished; it is transformed.

establishing connection of any kind between sensual practice and the dream, quite the contrary. It has happened to me—rarely, it is true— to have the most extraordinarily intense and extraordinarily beautiful dreams after orgasm. But also to dream a series of particularly remarkable and distinct dreams during periods of chastity and solitude. The connection escapes me, if there is a connection.

Also there is no rapport between dream images, properly so-called, and those of waking dream or the somewhat related hypnagogic visions or hypnagogic hallucinations, or yet again, erotic fantasies. Each of these closed-circuit systems has its own space, its own time, its characteristic rhythm and density. A group of images favored in one apparently never manages to insinuate itself into the other.

And yet, the way in which a narrative tale is formed within us, the choice of the episodes and the details, which never gives the impression of being a choice but rather a windfall that we sense is in no way fortuitous, and corresponds to the discovery of a precious object by an archeologist who has assiduously prospected an excavation site, and even more than this, the very rhythm of movement, certain dimensions and certain colors assumed by objects—shows us in the exceedingly attentive world of the creative imagination the equivalent of the proceedings of sleep. There are no exchanges between the two but analogies.

In *Fires,* all of "Achilles and the Lie," and more particularly the passage concerning the "spiraling descent" of the two characters the length of the twisting staircase from the tower is roughly the equivalent of a dream sequence; the same observation for the arrival of the barbarian hordes at the end of "Patroclus," which closely approximates the confusion, the oppressive crowding of certain dreams. Same observation for "Antigone"; the return of Antigone to Thebes, her search in the battlefield, Creon's race through the underground passages, the pendulum swing of the corpse inside the cavern are typical oneiric images, even though their formation was completely independent of dream. The intensity of the colors, forever fixed for me (if not for the reader) in the pages of "Antigone," also confirms the fundamental resemblance between this text [written] in the waking state and a [illegible word] of dream. Also same observation for certain passages of "Lena" where colors and dimensions stretched to an infinity of time and space are of the oneiric type, of the nightmare type. As for "Phedon," it is the smooth elision of images, fluid, quick transitions from joy to pain, unsurprised acceptance of untoward experience, and especially a certain blue color, the nuance of blue and rose coloration of the prison that place it in [illegible word] of dream. The *Coup de Grace,* which I had wished to anchor in the most solid reality, reveals its closeness to dream, finds its way within this register through a certain segmentation of reality, through the authority [an illegible word] of certain images— that of the staircase, for example, which recurs five times in the course of this brief narrative, allied to the presentation of a particularly significant moment in the heroine's life. Here the Freudian believes that he catches the dreamer in a sexual symbol and the occultist in a sacred symbol. Assertions without any trace of evidence. Nothing in context permits linking that staircase which Sophie sometimes climbs and sometimes descends to any sexual element whatsoever [the end of the leaf is scarcely legible].

Rough Draft, "Dreams"

[The beginning of this unpaginated, handwritten draft is missing, but the title was typed at the top of the first preserved leaf. The fragment compares modalities of dream and disincarnate experience after death.]

[lacuna] weightless world where one can wander endlessly without exhaustion, where objects no longer lie heavy in your hands, where one may observe food but not eat it, or not taste [excision] its flavor if one does eat, where one feels neither cold in snow scenes nor heat in jungle landscapes, where disquietude, sometimes fear, and, most often, easy acceptance of the absurd hold sway (as they do besides in life), but I am at a loss to find an example of anger or indignation, where one does not laugh and, if I were to believe in my own experience, does not hear laughter, where one sometimes sees weeping but does not oneself feel tears flowing from the eyelids, where one makes love without having previously experienced the excitement of desire, without the efforts and spasms of the bed. All things physical and carnal become light shadow in dream; in order to feel their weight and opacity again, it is necessary to leave the dream. What is there to say, if not that the kingdom where we spend our nights resembles, almost point for point, the land of the dead just as it is described for us in the sacred books of Egypt and especially in the extraordinary Tibetan *Bardo Thödol,* the most complete guidebook from beyond the grave. Disincarnated every evening, we serve the apprenticeship for our spectral state.

This leads me to discuss the role of the dead in our dreams. Everyone realizes that they figure less frequently than one would expect. The recent dead usually do not appear, no matter how ardently they are mourned and whatever the reasons for this customary absence may be. The older dead, however, do frequently appear, although their selection remains inexplicable. Apart from my father (but I will soon discuss at greater length the particular rapport with the dead forefathers in dream), none of the vanished whom I have most loved or grieved for has ever come to me in dream. Two friends, however, do appear there from time to time; one with whom I was closely tied for many years, but with an unruffled and somewhat dispassionate friendship without incident, which does not seem at first glance to be the most suited to awaken the powers of the imagination [unfinished]

On the Nature of Dream

[These three typed leaves are preserved in the Houghton Library. In guise of subtitle, they bear the mention, "Notes from 1969," although one of the annotations was apparently drafted in 1973. The following passages were probably conceived as a supplement to the preface published in 1938 and which the author refers to as having been written in 1936.]

In publishing the *Dreams and Destinies* of 1936 as it stands, I had always intended to append a few notes which might cast light on certain aspects of this text or would at the very least specify more precisely under what sort of conditions the oneiric experiments related therein were made. By a quite extraordinary stroke of good fortune, which is no doubt attributable to the fact that every claim asserted and every hypothesis offered in the 1936 preface had been the fruit of authentic personal experiences, I find nothing to excise or contradict among these reflections which are now aged by more than thirty years. But it does not seem inappropriate to me to amplify certain points with the reflections born of new experiences. It goes without saying that I have no intention of guiding the reader toward the ultimate truths of the oneiric adventure, but only toward a few roads of entry seldom frequented in this teeming jungle of dream that no one has ever explored in its entirety.

Dreams engendered in sleep must be clearly distinguished from the waking dream. Perhaps I had not sufficiently indicated that the some thirty narratives contained in *Dreams and Destinies* are authentically the sleeping woman's dreams. The period that immediately preceded the drafting of this book was also the only one in my life when, following the friendly advice of Edmond Jaloux, I systematically noted my dreams upon the moment of awakening. The fact that each of these narratives could just as well form a prose poem should not delude. This was in no way a question of poeticizing or embellishing the brute reality of a single dream but, on the contrary, of that almost desperate attempt, familiar to every proficient dreamer, of somehow managing to translate into words some modicum of the intensity of colors, the emotional complexity, the diversity of action in the dream. At worst, all of the words in the language would not be superfluous in order to more closely grasp the reality of a single dream. I concede to my interlocutor, but concede only after hesitation and rather grudgingly, that the waking dream could be insinuated into the editing of the sleeping dream, developing it or making it deviate from its original course. In point of practice, however, every awakened dreamer knows exactly where his nocturnal experience began and ended. If he strays in the least, he knows that he is lying. I do not deny that in certain cases a kind of hypnosis (let us not forget that this word derives etymologically from sleep) could seize the roused sleeper and cause him to continue his dream to some degree. By definition, such a state escapes observation by its subject, and so I cannot be certain of not having fallen into it.

And yet, no: every work executed in the state of waking dream betrays this fact by its formal characteristics, by a certain imprecision, or by a filiform slightness like that of spirit drawings and of which I find no trace in these narrations of dreams. And besides, it was not until much later, during those years that I can already label the last of my life, that the phenomenon of the nocturnal dream continuing in the form of the diurnal dream, providing the impression of living on several levels at once, began to happen to me. The dreams brought forth during those years of 1930–1936 did not pass across the frontier of awakening.

It was perhaps not obligatory in 1936 to signal that none of these dreams was the fruit of a hypnotic or hallucinogenic drug. This has become necessary in 1973. Those whom I call the true dreamers secrete their own drug. Hallucinogens are only for those who are incapable of penetrating their inner world by themselves.

If I had disposed of favorable circumstances and had an intelligent and bold medical attendant as my ally, I would have been tempted to try, just once in my life, a dose of a hallucinogen in order to compare the provoked visions to those visions that arise spontaneously. But I dreaded, by introducing a foreign agent into my inner world, even if just once, adulterating my future dreams in any way whatsoever. It is not for someone who hesitates to take an aspirin for an attack of rheumatism to use chemical substances for the soul.

What this vogue, grotesque as are all vogues, will have taught us is, nonetheless, invaluable. The evidence has been produced that the most obtuse of human beings has within himself architectures to rival Piranesi, celestial and infernal spaces worthy of Dante, efflorescences or braziers of colors akin to Asiatic painting or Turner, the swarming of monsters from Romanesque capitals. Better yet: now we know that the most commonplace of men is capable of feeling, under the liberating effect of a drug, the same anguish of limitless space that Pascal himself had experienced. The essential would be to search for a means of eliminating, without the aid of chemical products, the partition of ignorance, laziness, or fear that separates the man in the street from himself.

The outcome of the hallucinogenic experiences confirms those of the great natural dream on a point where the systems in vogue in our time have yielded up to a delirium of interpretation—namely eroticism. It is not surprising that a physician, Jewish and Viennese—Jewish belonging to an austerely Orthodox family in which all the sexual prejudices of ancient Judaism held sway; Viennese of the end of the nineteenth century, living and practicing in a society at once exaggeratedly lax and partaking on this score in all of the hypocrisies of the period—would have dealings with patients whose sexual obsession hid beneath the most grotesque disguises even in dream. By no means a historian—his *Leonardo da Vinci* and *Moses* prove it—Freud accepted as a universal truth what was only a circumstantial conditioning.

The dreams of a man or woman, unfettered in spirit and unfettered in morals, are much less encumbered with the residue of a frustrated sexuality. Freud's pansexualism was imposed because it corresponded to a profoundly natural reaction against the at least ostensible strictness of the moral world from which he emerged, and because a public eager to sport with its own frustrations sacrificed itself, so to speak, to the immense detriment of authentic eroticism.

Final Notes

[The following handwritten texts are found in a notebook that also contains, among other documents, footnotes for the preface to *Dreams and Destinies* dated 1983.]

Here, I record a note, the very idea of which would never have occurred to me before: none of the dreams were written under the influence of a hallucinogen. At the time of the first stir around mescaline and related substances, the thought did occur to me to try it once in order to verify for myself the difference between the spontaneous dream and the drug-induced or assisted dream. I did not do it.

The handful of individuals who actually read this book between the period when it was published and the present moment at which I am writing this note believed, for the most part, that the work was ultimately concerned not with precisely transmitted dreams, but with prose poems more or less freely contrived through the intermediary of dream. They were mistaken.

In order to retain its full savor, a dream must necessarily be narrated at length, leaving out nothing of its colors, its shapes, less frequently, the sounds and scents that combine to formulate this specific dream, unique in character. Most of the breakfast-table narrations told by the still sleep-laden people in our entourage distill a deadly boredom precisely because someone is offering us only a flat synopsis of the dream. In the insane and sagacious, futile and theatrical world of the dream, every single element counts and the dreamer owes it to himself not only to relate every detail, but to somehow convey to us the essential atmosphere in which the dream was enveloped. He must not omit even the dead leaf that stuck to the sole of his foot and which he is astonished not to find again between his sheets upon awakening. This is what I was attempting to do, even if the dreams, thus meticulously narrated, take on the appearance of a tale or a poem, which, in point of fact, they had during the dream.

The psychoanalysts, the psychologists, the erudite researchers into biographical subject matter, latch onto the dream: what a windfall for them. And who will contradict their interpretations? The dreamer herself realizes that almost every dream is inexplicable. The elements drawn from the dreamer's life, the daily life of the moment and the past life, are inextricable, more definitely arranged and differently assorted than in our memories, if we happen to have preserved some remembrance of them. Besides, the futile and the indifferent occupy as much or even more space in dream than does the essential, a perhaps humiliating truth that no dream analyst, whether certified with a diploma or working at the breakfast table, willingly accepts. The share of the futile and the indifferent in dream is like the share of chance in life; one either glosses over it in silence or else one exhausts oneself deriving symbols and metaphors from it. As in life itself, a great many dreams are set in places without interest, with chance characters whom we do not even recognize, too accessory to be perceived as friends or foes, or in any way as companions. And this intensifies the wonderment of the infrequent great dreams— wherein the insignificant, the incomprehensible, and the absurd also appear, but where something indefinable and splendid gleams inter- mittently like a precious stone, a meteorite arrived from another world, the furthest reaches of ourselves. Since I have undertaken to speak of their contents and form, I will seize the opportunity to express my amazement that no analyst of the subject has yet composed the sort of classification so frequently attempted for the poets' often decidedly less spontaneous metaphors. The centrality of architecture in the dream merits, in and of itself, an extensive study—and that it may signal an inherent faculty of the human mind is demonstrated by the fact that accounts of dreams owing to hallucinogens are also extravagantly endowed with architecture. From where does it arise, that entanglement of streets, lanes, staircases and porticoes, majestic or sordid squares, boulevards often as squalid as they are in reality, terraces that other staircases link to other terraces, hotel vestibules furnished with armchairs and porters, those complex arrangements, apparently scrupulously exact, of apartments where we have never been and which we have no intention of visiting someday? What to make of those colossal human termitaria with multitudinous floors and intricate corridors where identical doors open, leading to rooms yielding to other rooms, either empty or occupied by people whom we do not know? I remember, among other examples, a ride in an open hackney cab, neither tedious nor unpleasant but marked with a deliberate slowness that one finds in dream, through the confused meander of narrow streets in an Italian city of average interest. At last one emerged in a nondescript little square, facing a statue of Garibaldi, unless it was of another Risorgimento hero, whose name the coachman was declaiming. This ending that leaves us craving more might serve as the imagined conclusion of a short story or film, but, in my experience at least, the dream is unfamiliar with irony. Admirable, on the other hand, within a dream that I would label great for its extraordinary intensity of colors and forms, was the walk through streets lined with lofty, gothic houses of hanseatic type, black or red, weathered and muted brick, beneath a sky with low clouds, Nothing but a very beautiful urban landscape, uninhabited—no one was in the streets—and which led nowhere, except to the uppermost story of a house where a window-pane overlooked a canal. Scenery which could have belonged in one of my books, but which, until now, I have not placed in my books.

Some landscapes [several illegible words]

The plane and the horses.

The shore of the end of the world.

The temple of the end of the world.

Death's banner.

The block of ice on the roadway.

The visit to Michel.

The visit to the little cove.

The walk with a friend.

Variety of the figures. The figures seen. Names as labels.

The easy rapport between the living and dead.
Presence without presence (never in the dream).
(Absence of the intellectual vision or reasoning intellect.)

The dream's refusal to allow the major figures of our life or our works to enter.

The visits to the dead—rapport with Proust.

Refusal of the "scientifically" minded to accept color in the dream—sound, on the other hand, fairly uncommon.

Nonexistent taste. The awakening contact—which causes erotic dreams to have an abrupt ending.

The absence of enduring, obsessive figures.

Obsession—compared to the unexplained recollection of memory.

The intermittence of dreams. Perhaps a nonvalue.

Narration of Dreams

[These narrations, perhaps the sketches for the "commented dreams" that Marguerite Yourcenar mentions in her statement of intent of November 2, 1970, appear on seven typed leaves in the Gallimard Archives and on thirteen typed or handwritten leaves in the Houghton Library. These have been arranged chronologically, with the undated dreams at the end.]

The Green Grass

Night, 1961 (exact date uncertain)

[The narration of this dream has not been preserved. See "The
Visions in the Cathedral" and "The Wind in the Grass" in the original
sequence, as well as "The Promontories and the Islands" in the
following text.]

The Hippodrome in the Desert

Night of August 25-26, 1965

I have chanced to be in a vast desert plain, edged at the extreme horizon
by a chain of low blond hills. No village. No road. No tree. As far as
the eye can reach, the plain in its entirety was composed of the finest
red sand, crushed porphyry, of a single harmonious and warm color,
satisfying to the eye and to the mind. The ground, absolutely devoid of
any undulation, was perfectly flat, like that of a playing field, and, like
the sea, spread out to infinity. No wind, for not the least grain of sand
moved in that arena. Perfectly pure air. On my left, the lone building
visible in that tranquil vastness: an immense and long white house with
bare walls rough-cast in limestone, which obviously served as some sort
of inn or meeting place of distinctly Spanish or Mexican type.

Despite the absence of platforms, flagstaffs, gates, all of the usual
apparatus of racetracks, I realized that this place where I have chanced
was a hippodrome and that a race was imminent. On my right, a little
military band, made up of half a dozen uniformed men, buglers and
trumpeters. At their head, a man also armed with a trumpet, clothed
like the others in a banal uniform, vaguely navy blue. The man, who
had that placid and stolid look that one attributes to policemen, tells
me amiably: "I am going to do something to make them leave the
house." And he blew on his trumpet one sustained, clear note. At once

the crowd appeared, inquiring whether the spectacle was about to begin, and then trickled away, went inside.

But all of a sudden I noticed a transformation. Forms, which until now had been confused with the first spurs of the remote hills, had stirred: a long line of horses with dun, roan, or creamy white coats, mounted by riders arrayed in long garb of the same white or gently russet tones. A serene, mineral immobility once again held sway over the group that had advanced a few steps and then stopped. For the second time, the musician sounded a full, clear note. This time, the line advanced at a trot, an almost gilded cloud drawn over the red plain. At the head, a horse, this one jet black, but almost entirely covered, as if by a caparison, by the flaps of its rider's blond garb, started galloping and caracoled. I awakened, leaving behind a perfectly beautiful and pure world.

Dream of January 28-29, 1966

I no longer remember the beginning. I reside with Grace and apparently several other individuals in a house in the woods. A sort of dormitory upstairs.

Someone knocks on the door and it is our neighbor, who, as usual, has assumed the role of honorary letter carrier. He brings a large parcel of printed matter; Grace has gone downstairs to open the door and climbs up again with the parcel. I am anxious about her so needlessly exhausting herself.

The parcel contains admirable reproductions of drawings by Michelangelo, unknown to me until now: a profile of Cavalieri, a Garden of Olives, a Denial of Saint Peter. There is also a set of exquisite Chinese wash drawings depicting landscapes. We spread out all of this treasure upon a table of white wood and marvel. It so happens that these beautiful images were sent by a French visitor, a man of science who had come to work in the Bar Harbor laboratories and whom I had met by coincidence. It is too late to phone him, since he has already left again for Paris, but I determine to write to him.

Next, I find myself, in this same house, in a large room that serves both as an artist's studio and a kitchen, and, with the help of our jack-of-all-trades, Dick A., I am engrossed in modeling a large majolica dish adorned with fruits and vegetal motifs in the manner of Bernard Palissy. Very beautiful music (but I no longer remember a single note) fills the room. Within the room, there is a little cubicle with sides of ground glass set in a corner, which bears a strong resemblance to those private offices where senior bank employees are permitted to work without distraction. When Jay, the neighbor's son, parts the door a crack, I notice that a man of imposing stature, broad shouldered with beard already sprinkled with gray, has been introduced into this cubicle, where he plays the violin with admirable virtuosity. The child is cautioned to close the door again in order not to disturb the artist, but through the panes of ground glass we continue to observe his massive silhouette; he sways to the rhythm of the music and Jay points out that he resembles a great bear. Abruptly, he stops playing and leaves. For my part, I have gone into a lumber room to search for a little dish of heat resistant earthenware, purchased not long ago in France or in Portugal and which holds color crayons for my work, although it is more frequently employed for culinary purposes, for baking our various gratins. The lumber room is terribly crammed and Dick A. and I have a great deal of trouble locating the little dish and a box containing all the usual artist's paraphernalia, including tubes of oil color, and also great difficulty extricating them from the detritus shunted aside there. No doubt it was the noise we made that interrupted the musician.

I resume my modeling and clumsily let the little dish fall to the ground, where it breaks to pieces with a harsh din. At least I think that it is broken, but, when picking it up, I discover that it has suffered the fate of a book whose cover has become dislocated; two large fragments of clay remain hanging by the equivalent of fibers to the rest of the dish. I tell myself that a little wax will glue it all together and repair the damage, then I reflect that the wax will melt as soon as it is placed in the oven again. After all, it hardly matters to me whether or not it is broken.[*]

I should add that, at a given moment, a conversation of a rational type was taken up between myself and an unnamed person about Bernard Palissy and dishes with vegetal design in old Brusselsware and Portuguese ceramic. Also, at the opening of the dream, some quite pertinent reflections relating to the fact that the profile of Tomasso Cavalieri by Michelangelo "does not exist." The properly oneiric elements are the quasi-sacred beauty of the drawings and especially of the Chinese wash landscapes, which we gaze upon as you would actual landscapes glimpsed through a window, even though we are leaning over the table where they are outspread and contemplate them from above. Also oneiric, the benevolent majesty of the musician, his installation in the cubicle, and his silhouette that we continue to perceive through the ground glass, not unlike the way that I happened to glimpse the outline of a ringer sounding the bells through a leaded window in grisaille some years ago in a church in Shrewsbury (and I was so struck by those enlarged and blurred movements that I described them in *The Abyss*).

---

[*] [manuscript note at the bottom of the page, without reference to insertion in the text] Real elements: anxiety about G.'s health, the house in the woods, but *different*; the postman-neighbor; his son; the expert met by chance in Bar Harbor. (The drawings by Michelangelo are perhaps inspired by a luxurious volume of reproductions browsed at a local bookstore.) The little dish of heat resistant earthenware and the box with painter's paraphernalia. The encumbrance of the storage room.

Oneiric as well, and clearly genuine symbols of the soul and body conceived as two separate entities, and of longed for or anticipated death, the departure of the musician roughly synchronized with the breaking of the earthenware dish, irreparable and not regretted.

The Mass Suicide

Night of April 12-13, 1970

The most interesting aspect of this dream is that it is neither violent nor somber, although its theme is forbidding.

For vague and confused reasons, which seem to be connected with war and an inevitable invasion by enemy armies, it was decreed that the population of the region where I am found will commit suicide. Apparently, we are part of a floating population camping in a sort of vast and fertile plane: perhaps in dream I had thought of groups of refugees, but this scene is striking in its absence of all disorder and ferocity. Exceptionally tranquil people, outstretched on the grass beneath blankets, take poison or prepare to do so the next morning, after having spent their last night conversing in lowered voices or sleeping. After some time elapses, seemingly the equivalent of hours, I leave the group where I am found in order to reach the bank of a small pond, located some distance away. (Here, there is a gap in the fabric of the dream: am I supposed to bear a message or search for something?) Beside the pond, I am reunited with a friend unknown to me in the waking state, a young man in his twenties, of a pensive and, as it were, angelic beauty. He shoulders responsibility for this region where he is found. My dog cheerfully runs alongside the pond, and after several kindly caresses, I give him a powerful soporific, which I have also taken and which sends him into a pleasant sleep.

Leaving this friend with whom I was reunited, I set out for the seashore. While walking, I realize that I had overestimated my stamina:

my gait is faltering and I experience a kind of slight vertigo. Nonetheless, I continue along my path, but the scenery has changed: it has now become that of Mount Desert Island where I live, but with the one difference that the houses no longer exist. The road I follow is roughly the one extending from Northeast Harbor to Seal Harbor, and my goal is to arrive at the shore of this last locality in order to lie down beside the water, within reach of the tide which will sweep me out to sea. However, I realize within my dream that instead of carrying me away to the open sea, the waves might well bring me back to shore, but this hardly matters.

Suddenly, and with untold delight, at the bend of the road, approximately at the spot where in reality the ocean is found on the right and, on the left, when you come from Northeast Harbor, the hills and little lake of the Rockefeller property, I discover a horde of wild horses which come toward me, beautiful horses without saddles or riders, with roan or dun-colored coats. Some trot, other snort in sudden, graceful gallop. I awaken, filled with sensations of a sort of joy.

Attempted at dawn to go back to sleep in order to continue the dream but unremittingly found myself back at a period before its culmination, amidst the murmurs of the lowered voices and the silences of the night of vigil. Once again, details escape me; people tell me interesting things which I do not remember.

Dream of April 6, 1973

The dreams about my father, perhaps five or six in all, much in the spirit of Proust's about his grandmother (astonishment to learn that Michel is still alive; discovery that he is leading a greatly reduced existence, on the model of a poor worker's; cordial reunion but lacking great warmth; regret at having neglected him for such a long time and promise made to myself to visit him more often in the future).

Today, April 6, 1973, a very different dream apropos of him.

I resolve to go visit Michel, who is living somewhere at the seaside. By car (I am the driver), I follow a road running along the shore on one side, and, on the other, agreeably dominated by rocks planted with firs and other tall trees, discerned in silhouette against the night. The road is frost covered but one can move on. After a brief moment, however, it is closed off by an immense block of ice, glittering in the penumbra, completely white, more or less crooked, and with upper corners rounded because the ice has melted. (I supply these details in order to demonstrate the extent to which the block of ice is perceived in terms of pure realism.) Behind this block, let us say at twenty meters' distance, another, and yet another, and a fourth. Obviously, the car will not be able to continue. I backtrack. But how beautiful those blocks shimmering with whiteness beside the dark shores.

Night of April 9-10 (1973?)

My room being cold, I get up around 5 in the morning and look in at G.'s. I stretch out next to her and the dog in bed, without waking either of them. Sound sleep (that restorative sleep after severe illness). I dream that I am at work with H. on a radio broadcast (which has never occurred). The dialogue, of a poetic tone to my mind, is to be broadcast during the intermission of a fireworks display for a celebration in San Francisco (a city that I have never visited and never think about). In order to hear our work which is going to be played back to us, we lie down. As it so happens, we are both nude. Pressed close together but without carnal play. My head is on his shoulder. Without an orgasm, bliss floods me, that delightful repletion of sensual bliss, comparable to nothing else.

Night of October 13-14, 1973

I'm traveling pleasantly by train, in a sort of Pullman car, with a few likable strangers and a markedly courteous elderly lady who acts as my guide. We are crossing the Polish forests and I think to myself that it is high time to stand before the window in order to miss nothing of the landscape. Wondrous green depths. After some time has elapsed, our train moves onto a levee that follows the course of a large river, unless the train itself races over the water like a ship. The banks shaded with trees are crowded with great white oxen that swim and snort in the water, or peacefully lie there, slumbering. Gradually, emerging from the forest paths that lead from all sides to the river, a horde of white and pale gray horses also come to frolic in the water. Admirable awareness of the abundance and force of the world. Then the setting changes: I am in a car with my guide, driving through an unfamiliar city, most probably also Polish, very northern looking, at once sumptuous and austere with its large gabled wooden houses and its portals of sculpted stone. I get out in front of a sort of town hall in order to buy a few antique curios presented in a pushcart. The one I choose is a delicate glass bottle, in which I plan to pour the essence of mint (peppermint or rather wintergreen), which I use to massage my knuckles somewhat deformed with rheumatism. This very beautiful dream concludes on a comic note: someone announces the arrival of Mrs. P., a fine, bustling and peremptory individual whom I try to avoid as much as possible. It is time to get back in the car.

January 24-25, 1976

Extraordinary dream, not so much in and of itself, but because it seems to partially reveal the technique of dream. Set between half-past 6 and half-past 8 in the morning. Seems to have lasted for days on end.

Remarkable from the outset for a sense of euphoria. I'm enjoying a pleasant stroll with my spaniel, up and down the Champs-Elysées, then climb into a car with my father who takes charge of the dog. I return home on foot, that is to say, in this dream, back to the Hotel Saint-James, rue de Rivoli.

Before getting back, I decide to stop and buy the *Figaro,* a most uncharacteristic gesture on my part since I seldom read the newspapers. The wizened saleswoman to the right of the hotel objects to giving me a copy: "They are no longer fresh." But that need not be a hindrance and off I go down the bank toward the east, scrutinizing all of the shops, in quest of a news vendor.

I realize that the popular aspect of the street grows more marked: secondhand clothes shops, dealers in cheap lingerie and worthless antiques. At the end of a long block of buildings, I decide that it is high time to return home and I think that I remember the existence of a shortcut that opens into a side street.

The shortcut does, in fact, exist, but leads to a sort of wasteland, obstructed with the ruins of half-demolished buildings. The hotel gardener, who is weeding his flower beds beyond, greets me in a friendly way, but I attempt in vain to scale a little crumbling wall and prefer to circumvent these obstacles; in order to do so, I make for the right but a deep pond, where children are playing, prevents me from passing.

Once again, this need not deter me (the entire tone of this dream is light-hearted). I get back to the rue de Rivoli and find my way again to the spot where the door to the hotel should be. It no longer exists. (Here, the dream has a point of contact with reality: the hotel was closed this year for repairs.) I retrace my steps toward the right and find a pastry shop that appears to be of good quality; I inquire within if there isn't some sort of corridor to reach the hotel but am politely shown out by a young waitress with a fixed and feigned smile. Once again, we must retrace our steps. The wizened stationer and newspaper vendor already mentioned allows me to make a few purchases this time around and I leave by a door that should open into the rue Saint-Honoré and the other entrance to the hotel.

But I do not find myself in the rue Saint-Honoré, but in a densely populated quarter of an unfamiliar city, a mixture of old and new buildings, gardens and ramparts. Open shops; gilded, late afternoon sunlight. I walk for what seems to me to be hours on end, without finding my bearings and without really being worried about finding them, experiencing something of the indefatigable happiness of those long perambulations in my youth through Zurich, Munich, or Vienna. Several times, I intend to ask my way of some passer-by, but I do not speak their language and they do not look like people who would know. On one occasion I do speak to a lady dressed in tweed, quite elderly (does she limp a little?), with whom I converse for almost a mile without finding out where I am. Besides, it hardly matters to me. The predominant feeling is one of astonishment. Where does this energy, the alacrity come from? I notice that I hardly weigh on the ground. Without trace of anguish, I fully have the impression that this experience has lasted far too long and that I really must return home. I encounter a man in his thirties with a pleasant face; we are evidently discussing painting. He claims to be Renoir's son; I reflect that the ages in no way agree; he points with his finger toward a kind of ancient fortified castle and explains to me that his father's best works are housed there. I assume that we are in Russia and that a museum of the Russian state is in question. Then I leave my interlocutor in order to continue my walk. Little by little, I become absorbed in a growing awareness of my almost complete lack of gravity. Am I dreaming? If so, it is time to wake up. But I do not succeed, despite repeated efforts to open my eyes wide.

Finally, I lift my hand level with my face and bite it in order to see if I will experience some pain; I feel none at all. The matter must be cleared up. With my right hand, I take a penknife from my pocket and graze the left; no trace of pain or blood; I now experience a sort of passionate desire, more intellectual than emotional, to leave this disembodied state. I do not perceive how.

In a retired part of the city, abounding in hanging gardens that drape their branches over the tops of ancient walls, I meet a rather young woman in a white blouse, of congenial aspect, who is playing with children. Her type is rather southern. I tell her that I need her help. "Yes," she says, "and I know why you are asking me." She seats me on a couch and spreads a white sheet over my shoulders as if she were going to wash my hair. At that moment, I awaken.

But the sensation of disembodiment or, rather, perhaps the stupor at having lived in a state so different from the habitual persists, lingers for a minute or two, as if I were having difficulty reaccustoming myself to living in the wonted state. Could it not be that the dead also experience this shock? Once again, I am struck by an already frequent presentiment of analogy between the dream life and what might be the life from beyond the tomb.

In any case, this is the first time in the course of a dream that I have made an effort to leave the dream.

When I compare this dream to the one, far less astonishing, that I dreamed the night before, I ascertain certain connections. In both, there was *euphoria,* a sense of the alacrity of being and the recovered freedom of movement. Quite pronounced in the second dream, it is also present to a lesser degree in the first, in the satisfaction at no longer suffering from vertigo and in no longer feeling exhausted while scaling the steep counterrail that leads to the upper city. In both cases, there was a visit or at least a passage through a city, and in both cases, guests, rather vague characters, whom it was essential not to miss. I had forgotten to mention that in the second dream the notion of guests waiting for me plays an important role, but without anxiety.

Dream of June 4-5, 1979

In the state of anxiety and weariness that I am living this year, I note the poor quality of most of my dreams. Quite a number of erotic dreams (a great deal more than in previous years), well defined (but without baseness and without violence). It all happens as if the physical horror of G.'s illness needed to be counterbalanced in dream by a few moments of physical sweetness, in several cases with unknown men and women, and once, scandalously enough, with a man for whom in the waking state I believe myself to have only feelings of sincere regard. On the other hand, I notice quite a number of dreams of devastation and material disintegration: complicated household removals, houses in ruination, etc. I continue to believe, and more and more strongly, that some wise vital principle must control these dreams. But perhaps it is necessary to accept for the time being this sort of safety valve.

If I especially make note of the dream from June 4-5, it is because it was so strangely beautiful in its simplicity and filled me for several days' duration, in spite of all, with a kind of happiness and tranquillity. Notwithstanding a shared kiss, I hesitate to label this an erotic dream, but it is certainly a dream of love, at once agape and eros.

I am having a sojourn in the countryside, in a village surrounded by fields and groves. I stroll in the vicinity (and it is worth noting the joy of this quite free stroll taken in dream for a woman who has become incapable of walking long distances). A friend, apparently belonging to the same group of persons staying in the village, joins me. I do not know him in real life. A man in his forties, or fifty perhaps, tall in stature, slim and sturdy, but as if worn out by life; the eyes are intelligent, the face sunken and of a white gray. (There is also no question of resemblance to any of the characters in my books.) He is well dressed in a nondescript gray suit. We are obviously close friends, and we walk peacefully, without speaking, hand in hand. In a path hollowed between two hills with rocky walls covered with trees, we stop for a moment and turn toward one another for the sake of being locked in each other's arms. Sustained kiss that is beyond passion, without, however, actually denying or precluding its possibility. We are simply, and most deeply, one. The moment after, we resume our walk, which ends in the village where our friends are waiting for us (they appear, however, not to know the extent of our closeness), and the end of the dream turns to an agreeable festivity on the grass.

Another Dream, Summer, 1979

I am leaving with friends. We go to the open countryside to help some people they know turn the hay. My companions are rather indistinct: no one that I recognize in particular.

Gentle countryside beneath a somewhat gray sky. Plain with low hills; not many trees. Thick and verdant grass, not very high.

Soon, one of the members detaches himself from the group with me. This is a man of slim stature, somewhat indistinct; I am unsure whether he is young or of mature age. We walk together through the countryside, without speaking or speaking of things that I no longer recall. One of the hills along our path is traversed by a rather short tunnel with a level entrance (not unlike the tunnels that facilitated service between what were formerly the various pavilions of Hadrian's villa, but you had access to those, I believe, by descending one or two steps). The tunnel is scarcely dark, on both sides you see the open countryside. In the center, where reigns a certain dusk in which we are mingled, the man and I embrace lingeringly in silence, and this moment fills me with infinite beatitude, without trace of the sensual or in which all sensuality is, at least, dissolved. Unalloyed *Happiness*. Then we go out again and return to the fields where our friends are.

The Promontories and the Islands

A vast land seen as if from above or from afar: gently flowing region, almost flat, without rocky elevations, without trees, without dwellings, without roads, from which the long promontories extend toward the sea. The sea itself is quiet, though lightly quivering, softly waved. All terrestrial portions of the landscape are covered over with thin short grass, more like moss or lichen, beneath which you can guess the poverty of the bare soil, but there is an unusual delicacy to this light facing of very pale green, slightly yellowish and veering to gold in places. A bay is hollowed between the two longest promontories; a group of islands seemingly welded together, whose hills have the same imperceptible undulations and the same pallid and gilded greenness as those of the terra firma, are set a bit farther away, at the edge of the ocean.

Landscape intensely alive in its solitude, where every point of the ground and the waters appears to breathe beneath a luminous, gentle sky barely brushed with mist. A vitality, an intense virtuality is scattered everywhere: neither joy nor sorrow, but a vague sense of beginning, almost of hope. As often happens to me with this sort of visionary dream, the image of these sweeping, vacant regions, to which I am unaware of any true equivalent, persists, superimposed on waking, through all the actions and aspects of the day, and endowed with greater reality than the latter themselves. Sites where I have lived, the dreamer confusedly wonders, or sites where I am going to live?

The Black Banner

I am lying in bed in my room, in the bed and the room where my sleeping body is indeed to be found. The door to the house gradually opens and people climb the staircase to the accompaniment of solemn music. Others climb the back stairs (in fact, the house has these two staircases) and reunite in my room. The leader of this crowd bears a black banner with white stars. His garb resembles that of a deacon in a medieval painting. He leans over my bed and lightly touches my face with his black banner. I awaken with the sense that I must welcome these strangers, silently gathered around my bed, with an attitude of graciousness and good will.

Diverse Documents

[The list of authors and literary or philosophical texts reproduced below is found on a single manuscript leaf.]

From Goethe to Hofmannsthal (Béguin).

Peter Ibbetson

Heraclitus.

Montaigne.

Freud.

Polemon.

The theme of the awakened dreamer (*Thousand and One Nights,* Shakespeare, Pascal, Chinese philosophy).

Roger Caillois.

Notes to Be Made and Comments

[The following are taken from plans for notes found on three handwritten leaves. Grace Frick's comments are reproduced in italics.]

A *dedicated copy, dated June 14, 1951 to the comtesse de Beylié du Moulin, 198, avenue Victor Hugo, Paris, XVIe:* "To the comtesse de Beylié du

Moulin, this book born long ago of a constant study of dream and encouraged by countless conversations with Edmond Jaloux, who delighted in frequent visits to this same nocturnal world." Marguerite Yourcenar, 1951. *In point of fact, this book never had a printed dedicatory inscription, but only an epigraph taken from Heraclitus of Ephesus (Solovine's translation). M. Y. did not have the Greek text and did not consult the original at that time.*

At the end of the preface, M. Y. added a note in pencil: It would have been necessary to discuss the slight, but unavoidable deformation that literary transcription imposes on a form of expression not based on words. (1951).

Concerning a System of Dreams

[Four undated, typewritten leaves entitled, "Concerning a System of Dreams and Yogic Exercises" are housed in the Houghton Library at Harvard University. Those passages concerning dream, sleep, and awakening are reproduced below.]

[Translator's note: Supplementary passages not included in the Pléiade edition, reproduced with permission of the Marguerite Yourcenar estate and the Houghton Library, are marked with a cross (†). After the excerpt presented below, the document concludes with the author's reflections on yoga meditation practices and their benefits.]

Endeavor to reexamine your dreams in the morning in order to know how your night flowed away. To the best of your ability, avoid reconsidering them further during the waking hours. The memory of a dream is akin to a state of trance that is still or is once again the dream. It is natural for a little mist to float in the morning or the evening sky, but prefer the clear sky at noon.

And yet, some dreams are so beautiful and majestic that they remain with you like your guardian angel. They are one of your moments of eternity.

Evil dreams do exist. Violence, hatred, indifference, disdain. Beware but admire them. Here, incarnated in symbols more beautiful than any you could have invented, is the worst part of yourself.

Erotic dreams. I seldom have them and the most uninhibited possess a serene and delicious innocence. Above all, they have taught me about the varied possibilities of my nature as a woman.

†It is only in novels, in my opinion, that an old man is able to recognize himself as a child in dream. I also find it inconceivable that a woman has ever dreamed of being a man, or the reverse. I have also never dreamed that I was an animal. A certain number of physical coordinates continue to exist in dream.

†Admonitions—Attempt to fall asleep naturally every evening by cultivating the method you find easiest (the easiest for me consists of growing weary while repeating to satiety lists of dynasties, geological nomenclature, grammatical exceptions, whatever serves: Choose a material without importance for you, or with little emotional significance, and in which some chance word or name will not throw you on the trail of the usual subjects of your reflection during the day. This is unavoidable for all of us in times of great distress; then attempt to *confuse* the trails.) The great commended methods—the Hindus' emptying of thought, Catholic examination of conscience or of the day's actions, meditation of a religious or cosmic order are very good exercises before falling asleep, and not in order to *fall asleep*.

†Erotic thoughts. You will encounter them from time to time. Do not be made uneasy by this straw fire, but warm yourself there, if you so desire. In some cases of weariness or extreme sadness, these phantasms do as much good as the performance of a lovely ballet or a concert of graceful music. In extreme affliction or extreme bitterness, it is, on the contrary, rare for them to show up, or if they do, for you to be able to welcome them.

NOLUIT CONSOLARI.

Dream landscapes. Provoked hypnogenetic visions. Do not count on these for falling asleep. They usually are not manifest until the moment when sleep has already almost begun.

†Drifting off in reverie—I am not very capable of this. Reminiscence of blissful moments or of beautiful, beloved places. The misfortune is that there are no blissful moments or beautiful, beloved places without some association with the memory of a sorrow, of an indignation, of an object of pity, a dissonance within the consonance. If I evoke St. Mark's in Venice in order to gently fall asleep to the spectacle of its gold, the notion of a Venice corroded with pollution arises. If in the indolence of pre-sleep, I again wander through Constantinople with A. E., behold, the syphilitic beggar immediately reappears. And each time, the preparation for sleep is over—and sleep for the night.

The colors of objects in dreams resemble those colors assumed by certain rocks when subjected to infrared light. Or are such as only certain great painters have made them gleam. Or yet again, such as were, no doubt, the colors of alchemical nomenclature. Their only rivals in intensity are certain shades of the dawn and the setting sun.

†I suggest that you pray every morning upon awakening and in your own manner. This may be useful for emerging from the dream, in case of need. It transpires that I repeat the admirable phrase from a psalm: "This day is a day that the Lord has made." It is also not amiss to pray for all creatures who have died or suffered while you were asleep. And as for good resolutions, beware of those slippery paving stones. Set yourself in a condition in which good resolutions are unnecessary.

†I do not count as a good resolution the simple reaffirmation of the discourse, the recitation of the Buddhist sutra that you have adopted for your practice: "As many as my faults may be, I shall strive to combat them. As difficult as study may be, I shall apply myself to study. As inaccessible as wisdom may be, I shall endeavor to attain it. As numberless as the creatures in the universe may be, I shall work to save them."

†And repeat now and then, throughout the day, separately, and whenever the occasion arises, one or another of these affirmations. But do not recite anything mechanically, with legs crossed on your carpet. You are not always worthy of formulating such an affirmation. You have nothing to gain by doing it lip service, through fatigue or distraction. May it, nonetheless, always be diffused within you.

†Discipline of getting up. There is something beautiful about leaving sleep and the dream behind just as you leave a bath, and immediately doing your physical exercises for limbering. And yet, this should not degenerate into a display of strict discipline or of rigorous self-mastery. If you are too tired to stand with your head down, renounce. Your body knows better than you what it needs.

†In case of illness or of extreme fatigue, certain methods recommend doing physical exercise *mentally*. The results are inestimable. But do

not set forth imagining that these mental exercises are accomplished without hard work.

†The claims of the yogis are extravagant. And even if they were not, they do not concern you in the least: it is not for you to expect that *siddhis* will be obtained from your modest beginner's efforts. It remains that they are correct in asserting that any individual who has complied, briefly though it may be, and even with the most meager results, with their physical and mental system, is forever transformed by it. He has discovered the existence of a more certain balance, gained awareness of certain inexhaustible powers. If all it takes to reach this rudimentary level, but definitively acquired, is to perform a few minutes of mental training for several years, who can say what the person who has consecrated a good portion of his life might attain? Yoga is much like the piano, where you can only timidly decipher a page of Bach, and even then in a simplified version, which is, nonetheless, already a tremendous accomplishment. That is no reason to deny the existence of virtuosi.

The Dream Alphabet of Mitelli

[Translator's note: The following clipping from a sales catalogue with the typed inscription "cat. 312, Salloch, 1974" and heading typed in French "Dreams and Destinies," with two typed lines crossed out beneath, is provided as a supplement to the Pléiade dossier. The document is reproduced with the permission of the Marguerite Yourcenar estate and the Houghton Library where it is housed.]

The Dream Alphabet of Mitelli (Mitelli) Alfabeto in Sogno . . . Folio, vellum, Bologna 1683.

A fantastic book. Each plate illustrates a letter of the alphabet, in a sort of dream vision. The letters, in the form and shape of animals or human figures, grotesque and realistic, allegorical, enigmatic, mysterious, are in the center of the page. They are surrounded by sketches of heads, hands, parts of the face, eyes, noses, and other things, some of symbolic meaning and some merely playful, and unrelated or related, like things in dreams. The drawing is of exquisite beauty. In the preface to his pupils, Mitelli reminds them to see not only with their eyes, but also with their minds and their inner eyes, and therefore he gives them this alphabet of "fantasmi e confuse imagini" which are, at the same time, models for designs of perfect harmony and proportion.

"The Dream" by Jean Bernard

[The dossier of *Dreams and Destinies* contains the article by Jean Bernard which appeared in the *Revue des deux mondes* of December 1976, pp. 557-66. The following paragraph was marked by Marguerite Yourcenar.]

"The newborn, whether kitten or human baby, must need repose in a state of paradoxical sleep for long periods, and, therefore, probably dreams considerably. The nursling apparently smiles in dream several days before smiling while awake. Eminent researchers are even at the point of establishing that, at least in certain species, the fetus dreams during its intrauterine life, dreams hidden in the womb before coming into the world. Perhaps these fetal dreams represent a kind of apprenticeship, a rehearsal of the movements that will be necessary for the impending birth."